WORLD WAR II

WORLD

US TROOPS PARADING THROUGH PARIS, FRANCE, IN 1944

WAR II

Scholastic Inc.

Flying Fortresses

An American B-17 bombs a chemical and oil works in Germany, on September 29, 1944. The bomber's nickname, the "Flying Fortress," was due to its carrying machine guns for protection and its overall toughness. It had an advanced bombsight for accuracy in daytime raids. B-17s flown by the US Eighth Air Force saw some of the fiercest fighting of the war.

Written by Sean Callery
Consultant: Terry Charman, Senior Historian,
Imperial War Museum, London
Art Director: Bryn Walls
Managing Editor: Miranda Smith

ISBN 978-1-339-03425-6

10 9 8 7 6 5 4 3 2 1   24 25 26 27 28

Printed in China   68

This edition first printing 2024

WOMAN WORKING ON A VENGEANCE DIVE-BOMBER, TENNESSEE, 1943

" **There is no blinking at the
fact that our people, our
territory, and our interests
are in grave danger** "
—FRANKLIN D. ROOSEVELT, DECEMBER 8, 1941

Contents

A show of strength

By 1944, the German army had installed
a string of enormous guns, like this one,
along France's Atlantic coast. They were
put there to defend the territory that
Germany had captured across Europe.
By then, the most terrible war in history
had also seen conflict in Africa, Asia, and
the Pacific. Countries fought to protect the
freedom of their people, lands, and ideas.

Destroyed cities

In World War II, families and children suffered as never before. Hundreds of cities and towns were turned to rubble as battles were fought in, around, and above them. This picture was taken in Saint-Lô, northern France, in July 1944; the scene was similar in Stalingrad, in the Soviet Union, or Warsaw, in Poland, or Dresden, in Germany.

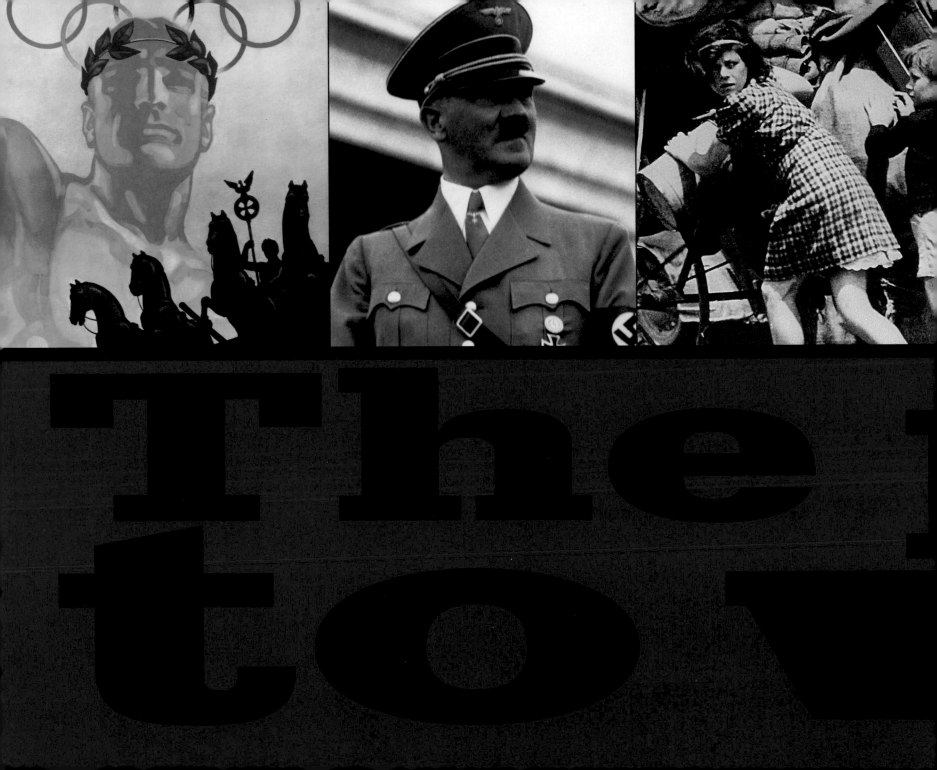

* What spectacle took place
in Berlin in 1936?

* Who led Germany–and
the world–into war?

* What was life like for
wartime refugees?

path
war

Road to war

In the 1930s, militaristic regimes ruled in Germany, Italy, and Japan. Their citizens wanted strong leaders to solve economic problems arising from a worldwide slump and, in Germany, hard conditions imposed by the peace treaties following World War I.

JAN. 1933
Adolf Hitler
Hitler, leader of the Nazi Party, seized power from President Paul von Hindenburg. Hitler was popular because he promised to make Germany great again. He immediately began to build up the country's army and weapons.

HITLER WITH HINDENBURG

JULY 1914–NOV. 1918
WWI
This appalling conflict in which 15 million died was a victory for Britain, France, Russia, and Italy over the German and Austro-Hungarian empires. The victors used the Treaty of Versailles to force Germany to disarm, give up lands, and pay vast sums of money.

ALLIED SOLDIERS FIGHTING IN THE TRENCHES

SEPT. 1931
Japan invaded Manchuria, on the east coast of China, to gain vital territory and minerals.

MAR. 1936
Hitler introduced military conscription—against the terms of the Treaty of Versailles, which had limited his army to 100,000 troops.

•1920• •1930•

Dots represent yearly increases until 1939.

OCT. 1922
In Italy, Benito Mussolini, leader of the National Fascist Party, marched on Rome and seized power.

JAN. 1924
In the Communist Soviet Union (now Russia), Vladimir Lenin died. Joseph Stalin took control.

OCT. 1935
Eager to gain territory in Africa, Italy used powerful mustard gas to help it conquer Abyssinia (now Ethiopia).

MAR. 1936
When German troops entered the Rhineland, on the border with France, no one tried to stop them.

OCT. 1929
The crash
The collapse of the New York Stock Exchange on Wall Street triggered the Great Depression, an economic slump that spread across the Western world. Millions lost their jobs and savings, and Germany suffered badly.

CROWDS PANICKING ON WALL STREET

JULY 1936
Trouble in Spain
When the Spanish Civil War began, Hitler and Mussolini helped the nationalist general Francisco Franco to victory. The German air force carried out the first large-scale bombings of civilians and destroyed the Spanish town of Guernica in 1937.

FRANCISCO FRANCO
Dictator, Spain

In power:	1936–75
Party:	Nationalist

AUG. 1938
The Spitfire enters service
Britain began building large numbers of this speedy, single-seater fighter plane. War was clearly coming, and control of the skies would be vital to defend the island nation from

PRIDE OF
THE RAF:
THE SPITFIRE

NOV. 9–10, 1938
Kristallnacht
The Nazi regime brutally oppressed political opponents and minorities, particularly the Jewish people. Kristallnacht ("Crystal Night") is named for all the shattered glass left on German streets after a night destroying Jewish property. This event is sometimes called the "November pogrom."

CLEANING UP AFTER
KRISTALLNACHT

JULY 1937
Japan used conquered Manchuria as a base for its ruthless invasion of China.

MAR. 1938
Hitler took over the neighboring nation of Austria. Again, no one challenged him.

APR. 1939
Italy invaded Albania. Mussolini was copying Hitler's aggressive empire-building strategy.

SEPT. 1939
France, Britain, and the Commonwealth countries Australia, New Zealand, South Africa, and Canada declared war on Germany. The US stayed neutral.

1939

OCT. 1936
Germany and Italy signed a treaty of friendship, known as the Rome-Berlin Axis.

Dots represent monthly increases during 1939.

FEB. 1939
Germany launched a massive battleship, the Bismarck, displaying to the world the power of its navy.

AUG. 1939
German-Soviet Pact
Germany and the Soviet Union agreed not to attack each other, and secretly divided Eastern Europe between them. Germany broke the terms of the Munich Pact and invaded Poland on September 1.

GERMAN TANKS IN POLAND

SEPT. 1938
Munich Pact
Eager to avoid a war and to support an enemy of Communism, European leaders allowed Hitler to occupy part of Czechoslovakia. The British prime minister, Neville Chamberlain, called the deal "peace for our time."

NEVILLE
CHAMBERLAIN
Prime minister, Britain
In power: 1937–40
Party: Conservative

38 million:
the number of gas masks
given out in Britain
a year after the Munich Pact

Rise of Nazi Germany

The Treaty of Versailles (1919) saw the victors of World War I strip Germany of land and demand huge payments as punishment. This damaged the German economy, and unemployment rose. Adolf Hitler offered an answer, promising to create a new German empire.

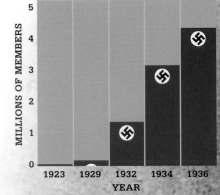

Bid for power

Hitler's National Socialist Party, often called the Nazi Party, tried to seize power in 1923. Hitler was found guilty of treason and spent eight months in jail. There he wrote *Mein Kampf* ("*My Struggle*") and outlined his belief that Germany must seize new lands.

Party membership
Germans believed that Hitler would make their country great again. When the Nazi Party gained power, it controlled who received the best jobs. To gain government employment, one had to join the party. Those who didn't became outsiders.

Military beginnings
Born in 1889 in a German-speaking part of Austria, Hitler hoped to be an artist. But he always admired Germany and eagerly signed up to fight on its side in World War I (1914–18).

Play money
When the German reichsmark currency collapsed, children played with stacks of banknotes that had no value.

Worthless money

In 1923, the German monetary system fell apart. The United States aided its recovery with enormous loans. But in 1929, the US economy collapsed with the Wall Street Crash. The US government was forced to call in all of its loans. The resulting worldwide Great Depression hit Germany especially hard.

Nazi Germany: Time line

Sept. 1919 *The army sent Hitler, now a corporal, to spy on extremist groups. He joined the German Workers' Party, forerunner of the Nazi Party.*

July 29, 1921 *Hitler became the Nazi leader and took the title "Führer." His rousing speeches attracted large crowds.*

Nov. 9, 1923 *Hitler failed in an attempt to overthrow the government. At his trial, his speeches received a great deal of publicity.*

Apr. 4, 1925 *The Schutzstaffel (SS) was formed. It was led by Heinrich Himmler, who later ran the Gestapo, or secret police.*

Hitler takes over

In January 1933, after an election with no clear winner, German president Paul von Hindenburg appointed Hitler chancellor, leading a multiparty government. But Hitler used emergency powers to take over running the state. When Hindenburg died in August 1934, Hitler became president.

Hitler Youth
German children had to join a Nazi youth organization. They were taught to love Germany and hate Jews and Communists.

The Third Reich

Hitler created jobs by strengthening the army and starting new building projects. He wanted to establish an empire known as the Third Reich (*Reich* means "empire"). The previous ones had been the Holy Roman Empire (800–1806) and the German Empire (1871–1918).

Flag for the new empire
The German flag was black, red, and yellow. In 1935, a new flag combined the red, white, and black colors of the Second Reich, plus the Nazi swastika (see page 20).

Technology
Hitler funded research on new military technologies. Scientist Wernher von Braun's work in the 1930s led to a pioneering rocket missile, the V-2.

Transport
Hitler ordered the design of a Volkswagen ("people's car")—an affordable car for German families. The first ones were rolled out in 1938.

The Berlin Olympics

The 1936 Summer Olympics were held in Berlin, the capital of Germany. Nazi dictator Hitler used them to showcase the military efficiency of his nation. The 49 competing countries did not challenge Hitler then or in the years that followed, even when he invaded neighboring countries.

No one wanted to provoke a war.

Jesse Owens

The hero of the Games was African American athlete Jesse Owens, who won 4 gold medals and broke Olympic records. His triumphs included defeating German star athlete Lutz Long in the long jump. Hitler was furious that an "inferior" person had defeated a white person.

Appeasing Hitler

The major European powers were worn out by war. Many thought that the reparations imposed on Germany in 1919 were harsh and that, like them, Hitler opposed Communism. They allowed Germany to invade Austria and, in late 1938, signed the signed the Munich Agreement.

Munich accord
Hitler and British prime minister Neville Chamberlain shake hands in Munich, 1938.

On the podium
At the medal ceremony, Long (right) gave a Nazi salute during the playing of the US national anthem.

Czech invasion

The Munich Agreement allowed Hitler to take over part of Czechoslovakia. The conquest of the rest of the country then became Hitler's goal. In 1939, German troops marched over the border. The other European powers suddenly realized that they could no longer trust Hitler.

Conquered city
The name of the Square of Liberty in the Czech city of Brno is changed to Adolf Hitler Square.

Nazi Germany: Time line

Mar. 7, 1936 *German soldiers marched into the Rhineland, bordering France. They met no opposition.*

Nov. 25, 1936 *Germany and Japan signed the Anti-Comintern Pact against the Communist Soviet Union. Italy joined in 1937.*

Mar. 12, 1938 *German troops march into Austria, breaking the Treaty of Versailles. The other western powers took no action.*

Sept. 29, 1938 *Hitler promised not to invade other lands if he was given part of Czechoslovakia in the Munich Agreement.*

Two weeks before the Games, top German high jumper Gretel Bergmann was dropped for being Jewish

Crowds salute Hitler
Hitler used the Berlin Games to gain popularity in Germany and to promote his image around the world. Huge crowds showed their support with salutes and chants of *"Sieg Heil"* ("Hail to victory").

Mar. 16, 1939 *Germany occupied the rest of Czechoslovakia. Again, other western powers did nothing to stop him.*

Aug. 1939 *Germany and the Soviet Union signed a nonaggression pact. They agreed to share Poland between them.*

Sept. 1, 1939 *Assured of Italy's support, Germany invaded Poland. Britain and France responded by declaring war on Germany.*

Ideologies

During the 1930s, a number of very different (and sometimes opposing) ideologies, or belief systems, were developed around the world. These differences eventually led to war.

FASCES

Fascism

Fascism is named after the fasces, an ancient Roman symbol of authority and power. Fascists value leadership and expect a dictator, or powerful ruler, to tell the people what to do.

Key points

Origins:	Fascist ideas spread from France in the 1880s
Children were taught:	The state is best
Led by:	A dictator, so that there are no disputes
Most influential group:	The military, to protect the state and suppress opposition
Opposed to:	Communism

BENITO MUSSOLINI

Lived:	July 29, 1883– April 28, 1945
Led:	Italy (1922–45)
Nickname:	Il Duce ("the Leader")

Fascist Italy

Italy and Benito Mussolini
In 1922, Mussolini and his followers, the Blackshirts, marched on Rome to take power. He became dictator in 1927.

SWASTIKA

Nazism

Nazis were fascists who also believed in the superiority of Aryans (a race of white people supposedly better than others) and thought they were born to rule over non-Aryans. Their symbol was the swastika.

Key points

Origins:	Hitler put forward the founding ideas of Nazism in his book *Mein Kampf* (1925)
Children were taught:	The Aryan race is supreme
Led by:	A dictator
Most influential group:	The military, to expand the German state and form a new empire called the Third Reich
Opposed to:	Anyone who threatened their ideals

Nazi Germany

Germany and Adolf Hitler
Even though he was Austrian, Hitler believed that the Aryan master race should build a new German empire.

ADOLF HITLER

Lived:	April 20, 1889– April 30, 1945
Led:	Germany (1933–45)
Nickname:	The Führer ("the Leader")

"What we have to fight for is . . . the freedom and independence of the Fatherland"
—ADOLF HITLER

"The people do not know what they want. . . . I have stopped the talk and the nonsense. I am a man of action"
—BENITO MUSSOLINI

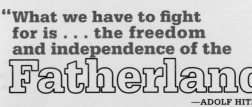

Two dictators
Hitler (center) and Mussolini (left) were allies but did not fully trust each other.

Communism

HAMMER AND SICKLE

According to Communism, all property and businesses should be owned by the people. Its hammer and sickle symbol represents industry and farming, showing that factory workers and farmers can work together.

Key points

Origins:	Karl Marx developed the idea of Communism in his manifesto in 1848
Children were taught:	No one has his or her own private property
Led by:	The Communist Party (often led by a dictator)
Most influential group:	Party leaders
Opposed to:	Capitalism (a free economy)

JOSEPH STALIN

Lived:	December 18,1878– March 5, 1953
Led:	Soviet Union (1924–53)
Nickname:	Vozhd ("the Boss")

Communist Soviet Union

Soviet Union and Joseph Stalin
The Soviet Union (or USSR) formed in 1922. From 1924, Joseph Stalin began to take over.

"From each according to his ability, to each according to his needs"

—KARL MARX

Democracy

BALLOT BOX

In democracies, people vote every few years for political representatives. Those with the most votes make, pass, or veto laws. Everyone has the right to express their own opinions.

Key points

Origins:	The ancient Greeks were the first known to elect leaders
Children were taught:	Freedom and equality are vital
Led by:	An elected official, like a president or prime minister
Most influential groups:	Lawmakers and voters
Opposed to:	Dictatorships

FRANKLIN D. ROOSEVELT

Lived:	January 30, 1882– April 12, 1945
Led:	United States (1933–45)
Nickname:	FDR

Democracy and the world
By the 1930s, there were many democratic countries, such as the United States, led by President Roosevelt, and the United Kingdom.

"As I would not be a slave, so I would not be a master. This expresses my idea of democracy"

—ABRAHAM LINCOLN

Militarism

Japan was led by Emperor Hirohito from 1926, but its real rulers were the heads of the army. Under this strong military rule, Japan wanted to expand into China and Southeast Asia, conquering European colonies to build its own empire. Japan's slogan was "Asia for the Asians."

Rising sun
This military flag shows rays coming from Japan's rising sun symbol.

Fighting for new lands
Eager to expand, Japan had fought and won against the Russians in Manchuria and Korea, from 1904 to 1905, and went to war with China in 1937.

Blitzkrieg

Germany conquered Poland in September 1939 with blitzkrieg ("lightning war") tactics. After an eight-month delay in military action—the "Phony War"—the Germans suddenly swept across Europe.

123 TANKS

Panzer (tank) division

A German tank division was made up of panzers and their crews, support staff, and equipment. The exact numbers varied, but a typical tank division in 1940 included:

1,402 TRUCKS **561 PASSENGER VEHICLES**

421 ARMORED VEHICLES **1,280 MOTORCYCLES**

394 OFFICERS **1,962 NONCOMMISSIONED OFFICERS**

9,321 SOLDIERS

Military buildup

Germany's quick victories were the result of years of preparation. From 1933 to 1939, Hitler increased the German army to more than a million soldiers. His air force grew from 36 to 8,250 planes, and his navy from 30 to 95 warships.

May 1940	Germany	Allies
Divisions	154	144
Armored vehicles	4,000	4,000
Fighter planes	1,100	1,100
Bombers	1,100	400
Dive-bombers	400	0

Opposing forces

The German army had more up-to-date equipment than the Allied forces of Britain, France, and Belgium did. The Allies' resources were also spread very thin.

French prisoners

1,575,600 prisoners were taken to Germany to work as slave labor.

Plans for expansion

Adolf Hitler planned to take over countries bordering Germany and use their "inferior" citizens as slave labor. He expected Britain to negotiate for peace.

Germany

Calendar days between invasion and surrender

INVADED: MAY 10, 1940
SURRENDERED: MAY 28, 1940

9

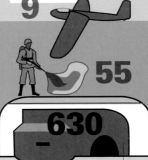

Belgium

After overpowering the 630 soldiers defending the strategic fortress of Eben-Emael, German forces rolled across Belgium. The capital, Brussels, fell in May.

BRUSSELS

BELGIUM

Eben-Emael

55

630

Capturing Eben-Emael

Gliders landed 55 paratroopers armed with flamethrowers to take this key Belgian fortress.

Ardennes Forest

INVADED: MAY 12, 1940
SURRENDERED: JUNE 22, 1940

PARIS

France

German tanks passed through the hilly, dense Ardennes Forest—to the surprise of the French. Pushing over roads clogged with terrified refugees, the invaders reached Paris on June 14.

FRANCE

Infantry
Foot soldiers carried machine guns or other hand weapons.

Motorized infantry
Trucks and other vehicles moved quickly into areas cleared by the tanks.

Bombers
Large bombers destroyed bridges, roads, and rail lines.

Tanks
These stayed in groups, so they had enormous firepower.

Dive-bombers
With their wailing sirens, these terrified troops and refugees.

SEPTEMBER 1, 1939

Lightning attacks

Blitzkrieg was a burst of fast, powerful attacks, designed to knock out the enemy. Dive-bombers screamed down on airfields, while tanks punched holes in enemy lines. Then the infantry surrounded the remaining, isolated defenders.

INVADED:
SEPT. 1, 1939
SURRENDERED:
SEPT. 27, 1939

WARSAW

POLAND

INVADED:
MAY 10, 1940
SURRENDERED:
MAY 15, 1940

INVADED:
MAY 10, 1940
SURRENDERED:
MAY 11, 1940

AMSTERDAM
ROTTERDAM

NETHERLANDS

LUXEMBOURG

LUXEMBOURG

Netherlands
German paratroopers were dropped in to smooth the way for the ground forces. After the Luftwaffe (air force) bombing of Rotterdam left 80,000 people homeless, the Dutch surrendered, fearing more attacks.

Luxembourg
With no army, neutral Luxembourg didn't stand a chance. It took just three hours for three German panzer divisions to rumble the 30 miles (48 km) across this tiny country.

Poland
Poland could not defend its long border against the Reich. Hitler had a pact to share Poland with the Soviet Union; Stalin invaded on September 17. Warsaw surrendered on September 27.

GERMAN   **POLISH**

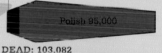
German 8,082
Polish 95,000
DEAD: 103,082

German 27,278
Polish 130,000
WOUNDED: 157,278

Heavy Polish losses
In the invasion, 12 Poles died for every 1 German. Nearly 5 times as many Polish people were wounded.

1,308

Deadly drop
The Germans dropped 1,308 bombs on the Dutch port of Rotterdam.

Paris, France
Hitler kept the capital under German control but allowed southern France to govern itself until November 11, 1942, when Vichy France was occupied.

Refugees
47,000 people fled from Luxembourg to France. They didn't realize that the Germans were heading there, too.

47,000

"The small countries are simply smashed up, one by one, like
matchwood"
—WINSTON CHURCHILL'S MESSAGE TO FRANKLIN D. ROOSEVELT, MAY 15, 1940

Refugees

The fighting and the threat of Nazi rule terrified millions of people who were in the path of the invasion. Many, like this French family, packed as many possessions as they could and fled on the dusty roads. Leaving behind homes, jobs, and normal life, refugees faced hardships and danger. Many were even attacked by German dive-bombers.

Theaters of war

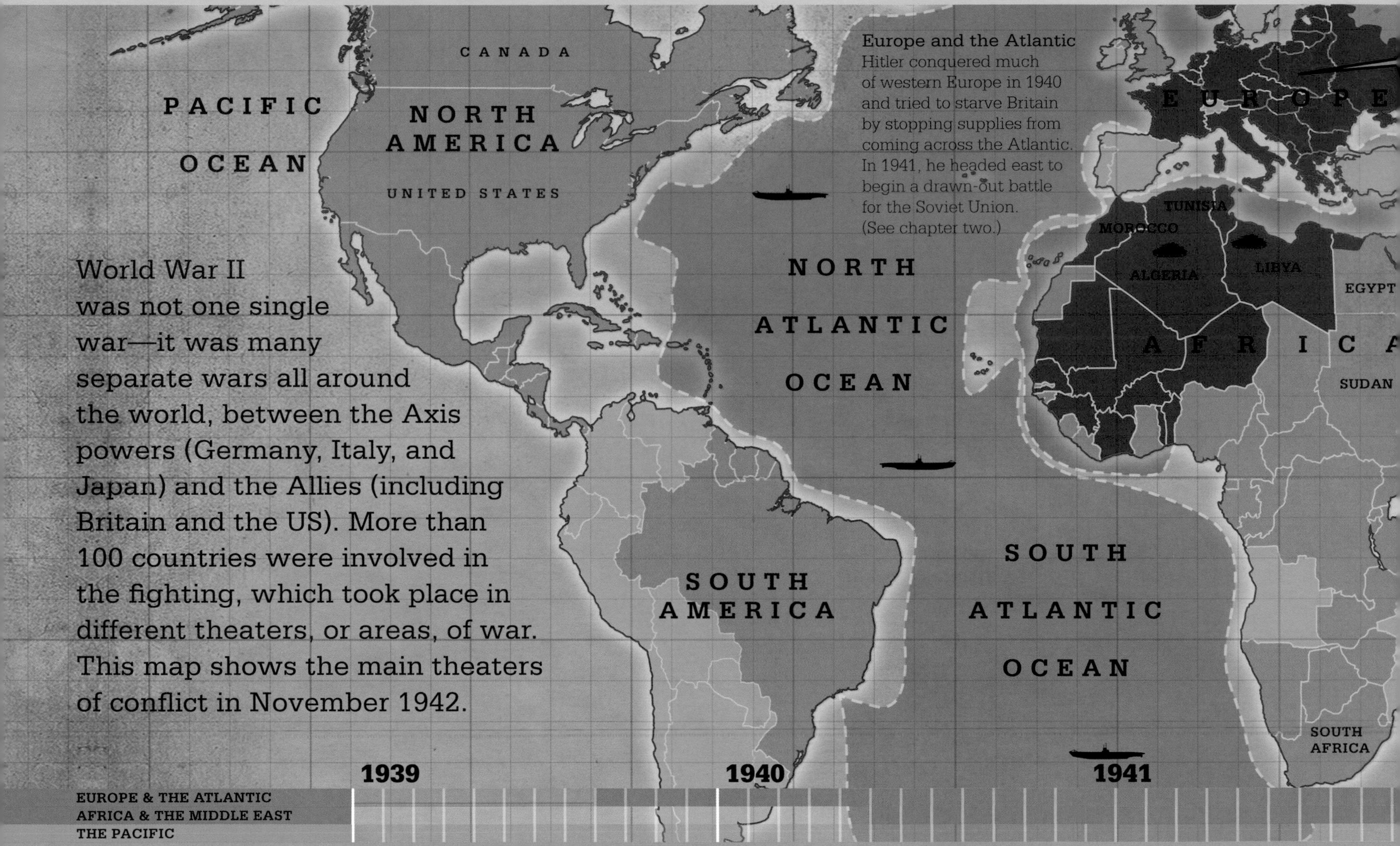

World War II was not one single war—it was many separate wars all around the world, between the Axis powers (Germany, Italy, and Japan) and the Allies (including Britain and the US). More than 100 countries were involved in the fighting, which took place in different theaters, or areas, of war. This map shows the main theaters of conflict in November 1942.

CANADA

NORTH AMERICA

UNITED STATES

PACIFIC OCEAN

NORTH ATLANTIC OCEAN

SOUTH AMERICA

SOUTH ATLANTIC OCEAN

EUROPE

AFRICA

TUNISIA
MOROCCO
ALGERIA
LIBYA
EGYPT
SUDAN

SOUTH AFRICA

Europe and the Atlantic
Hitler conquered much of western Europe in 1940 and tried to starve Britain by stopping supplies from coming across the Atlantic. In 1941, he headed east to begin a drawn-out battle for the Soviet Union. (See chapter two.)

1939

1940

1941

EUROPE & THE ATLANTIC
AFRICA & THE MIDDLE EAST
THE PACIFIC

Key events of the war
The Axis powers advanced from 1939 to 1942 but were slowly defeated, at a cost of millions of lives.

1940 *The British air victory in the Battle of Britain put a stop to Hitler's western advance.*

1941 *Japan's attempt to destroy the US Pacific Fleet in the naval base at Pearl Harbor, HI, brought the United States into the war.*

DEC. 1940
T-34 tank enters service
Soviet tank factories began building the T-34, one of the most effective tanks of the war. Enemy shells simply bounced off the sloping armor of these fast, powerful metal giants.

A SOVIET T-34 TANK

6 million: the number of European Jews killed in the Holocaust

DEC. 1941
The Holocaust
The Nazis opened the first death camp. Millions of Jews—whom the Nazis considered "inferior"—were killed in these camps.

JEWS ARRIVING AT AUSCHWITZ-BIRKENAU DEATH CAMP, 1944

SEPT. 1941
The German army sealed off the Soviet city of Leningrad and starved its people for 872 days.

OCT. 1941
The Battle of Moscow began as German forces threatened the Soviet capital.

MAY 16–17, 1943
British planes dropped bouncing bombs on German dams in the Dambusters Raid.

1941 **1942** **1943** **1944**

Dots represent yearly increases.

MAR. 11, 1941
The Lend-Lease Act allowed the US to supply Allied forces.

AUG. 1941
A young woman named Andrée de Jongh set up the Comet Line, a rescue route for shot-down Allied airmen.

MAY 30, 1942
More than 1,000 British planes bombed and destroyed the German city of Cologne.

AUG. 1942
The battle for the Soviet city of Stalingrad began. It lasted through the freezing winter.

APR. 19, 1943
Jews rebelled against the Nazis in the Warsaw Ghetto Uprising.

MAY 1941
Enigma
The British capture a functioning Enigma, a German encoding machine. Building on work by Polish intelligence, the British figure out how to decode German naval messages.

THE GERMAN ENIGMA MACHINE

JUNE–DEC. 1941
Operation Barbarossa
Soviet leader Joseph Stalin was horrified when Germany broke its peace pact. About 4 million German troops advanced into the Soviet Union as Hitler switched his attack to the east.

GERMANS ADVANCING PAST A BLAZING SOVIET TRUCK

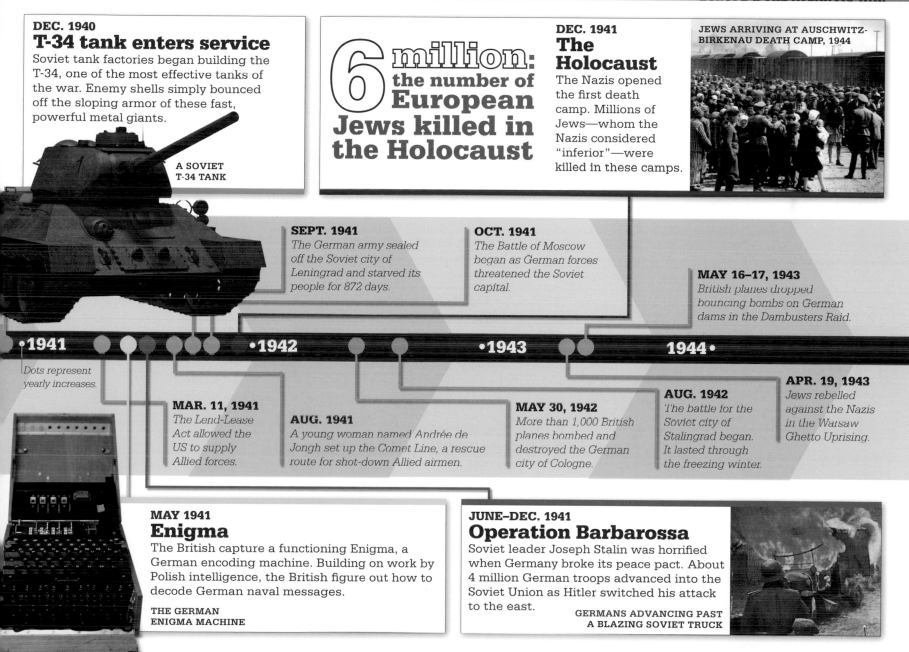

Hitler blocked

If Hitler wanted to invade Britain, he would first have to gain control of the skies over southern England. So the Luftwaffe sent its speedy Me 109 fighter planes to face British Spitfires and Hurricanes. The Battle of Britain was fought from July 10 to October 31, 1940.

Hurricane specifications	
Top speed	325 mph (523 kph)
Range	600 mi. (965 km)
Maximum altitude	34,000 ft. (10,365 m)
Wingspan	40 ft. (12 m)
Armament	8 machine guns
Number built	14,533

Hood
This was built from the newly invented bulletproof material Perspex.

Machine guns
The pilot fired the four guns by pushing a button in short bursts.

Propeller
Three metal blades sliced through the air.

Tail fin
The rounded tail fin and large rudder allowed the plane to make tight turns.

Tail wheel
This wheel did not tuck in during flight.

Dogfights

When German planes crossed the English Channel to attack British radar stations and airfields, Royal Air Force (RAF) pilots took off to intercept them. Groups of planes had deadly dogfights, performing desperate corkscrew turns and dives. Each tried to get behind an enemy plane and fire a blast of bullets or shells to rip it apart and send it spiraling downward.

Scramble!

Between fights, pilots tried to rest. Then the next warning would come in, and they would "scramble," running to their planes. Sometimes they flew five missions in a single day. Their biggest fear was being burned alive in a shot-down plane.

Hawker Hurricane
Hurricanes claimed more than half of the German planes shot down in the Battle of Britain. They could be rearmed, refueled, and ready to return to the skies in just nine minutes.

Wing
The aluminum covering was lightweight but strong.

Ready to fly
A British pilot wore leather headgear that had a built-in oxygen mask and radio.

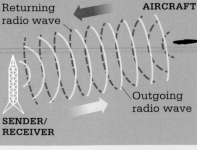

Returning radio wave

AIRCRAFT

Outgoing radio wave

SENDER/RECEIVER

How radar helped
Radar sends out radio waves that bounce back off objects such as planes. This vital tool allowed the British to detect enemy planes before they came into sight.

Me 109 specifications

Top speed	398 mph (640 kph)
Range	530 mi. (850 km)
Maximum altitude	39,370 ft. (11,880 m)
Wingspan	32.5 ft. (10 m)
Armament	2 machine guns, 1 cannon
Number built	32,984

"Never in the field of human conflict was **so much** owed by so many to so few" —WINSTON CHURCHILL

Pilot
The pilot's heated flying suit plugged into the cockpit.

Front cannon
Shells were fired through the propeller.

Engine
The fuel-injected engine was better at handling dives than that of a British plane.

Messerschmitt Bf 109
Known as the Me 109 for short, this sleek fighter could climb and dive faster than its British rivals, but it did not turn as well. The Luftwaffe relied on about 33,000 Me 109s.

Frame
The plane was made of thin, light metal to reduce drag.

Fuel tank
This held enough fuel for a flight just over an hour long.

Wing gun
Bullets for this gun were fed from the fuselage, to keep the wings light.

Wing
The wings were thin and light, with special slats that provided more control during dives.

Dunkirk

In late May 1940, the Germans had the British, French, and Belgian forces pinned down and at their mercy on the French coast, near Dunkirk. A rescue fleet was sent across the English Channel before Hitler had a chance to attack. The 861 boats ferried 338,000 troops back to Britain. They had to abandon their equipment but they were safe!

Little ships
Troops waded through choppy waters in their heavy uniforms to reach their rescuers. Small fishing and sailing boats shuttled the men to destroyers and other large craft.

The Blitz

For eight months after September 7, 1940, the Germans rained down bombs on Britain's cities. The Blitz left 43,000 people dead and 250,000 homeless. A night for a typical family might have gone like this:

6:00 PM Blackout curtains are closed so that lights inside the house won't help bombers find a target.

6:30 PM The family puts an emergency bag by the door. It contains a flashlight, candles, matches, blankets, ration books, gas masks, and ID cards.

8:00 PM The air-raid siren wails: Radar has detected bombers over the English Channel.

8:10 PM The family leaves the doors of the house open, to limit the effects of a blast. In the yard, they hurry down the steps of an air-raid shelter.

8:20 PM Antiaircraft guns clatter at the bombers, aided by searchlights. The family hears the whistle of falling high-explosive bombs and the wail of fire engines.

10:30 PM The next wave of planes releases high explosives, and the shelter rattles with each blast.

5:00 AM The two-minute "all clear" siren sounds. The family finds their house unscathed—this time.

7:00 AM The cleanup begins: sweeping glass, digging out bodies, and tending to the injured, while children rush to add to their shrapnel collections.

177,000
people slept on underground train platforms

Resistance

Across Europe, individuals risked their lives with small acts of resistance—such as cutting phone lines—against the occupying Germans. Soon these individuals banded together to become more organized groups.

Fighting back

Resistance groups fought back in many ways, from printing anti-Nazi leaflets to kidnapping or killing German officers. They also smuggled out information about targets the Allies should bomb.

SOE messages

Unoccupied Britain set up the Special Operations Executive (SOE) to support resistance movements across Europe and, later, in Japanese-occupied Asia. Its male and female operatives often parachuted in to help, organize, and equip these "secret armies," keeping in touch using covert radios.

Control switches
These set the volume and tone so that messages could be heard clearly.

Magnet
This attached the mine to a metal surface.

Sabotage

Members of the resistance made life harder for the German army by blocking roads, blowing up bridges and tunnels, and wrecking railroads. Damaging the transport system slowed down the movement of enemy troops and weapons.

Truck stoppers
Spiked caltrops were placed on roads to puncture the tires of vehicles in enemy convoys.

Clam mine
This mine consisted of high explosives and a powerful magnet, which was designed to stick to a bridge or rail line. It could be detonated remotely.

CLAM MINE   **DETONATOR**

Copper coil
This tuning coil was used to find the wavelength of incoming messages.

Headphones
These allowed radio operators to work without being overheard.

Suitcase disguise
This secret radio was made by the SOE for use in France. The case hid it from prying eyes, but it didn't make it easy to carry—it weighed 30 pounds (13.5 kg)!

Radio codes
Anyone could tune in to radio transmissions, so messages had to be sent in code.

Helping heroes
The resistance network gave food and shelter to airmen who had been shot down. Pilots usually trekked south to British-run Gibraltar for journeys home.

Resistance heroine
From Vichy, in central France, Fourcade led the Alliance, a network of 3,000 agents.

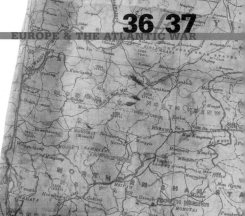

MARIE-MADELEINE FOURCADE

Code name: Hedgehog	
Lived:	1909–89
Resistance leader:	1941–45

Silk maps
Allied airmen were issued with silk maps to help guide them if they were shot down. Unlike paper, silk didn't rip or fall apart if it got wet.

"Who will ever suspect a woman?" —GEORGES LOUSTAUNAU-LACAU, THE MAN WHO RECRUITED MARIE-MADELEINE FOURCADE

Spare valves
Valves were tubes of thin glass that controlled the electricity supply.

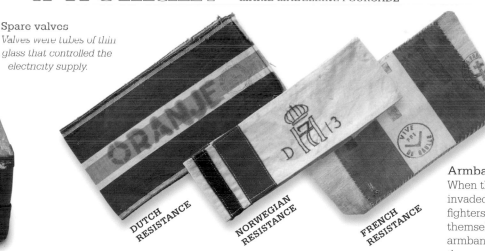

DUTCH RESISTANCE

NORWEGIAN RESISTANCE

FRENCH RESISTANCE

Armband ID
When the Allies invaded, resistance fighters identified themselves with armbands like these.

Batteries
These provided backup power in remote places with no electricity.

Morse tap
Tapping this produced two different clicks for sending messages in Morse code.

To resist or not?
There were resistance movements in every occupied country, but not everyone resisted. Most people simply waited out the war, while others collaborated with the Nazis.

The eastern front

On June 22, 1941, Hitler switched his attack from western to eastern Europe. He broke his peace pact with Stalin and invaded the Soviet Union with a force of 4 million troops. Hitler wanted to control the country's resources, rule its "inferior" peoples, defeat Communism, and kill Russian Jews. However, just six months later, the Germans were forced to retreat outside Moscow.

"It is the Führer's unshakable decision to raze Moscow and Leningrad to the ground"
—GERMAN SUPREME COMMAND, 1941

The invasion
The Germans advanced quickly, thanks to their state-of-the-art weapons. In just three months, they had killed or captured 3 million of the poorly equipped Soviet troops.

LENINGRAD
Sept. 8, 1941

MOSCOW
Oct. 13, 1941

GERMAN
ATTACKS

RUSSIA

STALINGRAD
Aug. 23, 1942

Operation Barbarossa
Hitler's plan was to capture and occupy the Soviet Union in the summer, when travel was easy on dry roads. Targets were major cities, oil fields, coalfields, and farms that could supply the Third Reich with fuel and food.

Divided attack
Germany pushed forward toward the key cities of Leningrad, Moscow, and Stalingrad. Its forces were spread too thinly to conquer them.

Turning the tide

The Soviet Union's Red Army fought out of pride for their country—and fear. Stalin had ordered that those who deserted or surrendered would be shot, and their families punished. Slowly, the Soviets pushed the Germans back.

Supplying the army
Stalin moved munitions factories east, away from the fighting. The laborers worked grueling 18-hour shifts to keep the army supplied.

Rifle power

Hidden Soviet snipers could fire on enemy soldiers up to 1,200 feet (365 m) away. They worked in pairs. One acted as a lookout, and the other fired shots. Then they swapped.

Girl power
About 2,000 Red Army snipers were young women.

Weapon of choice
The Mosin-Nagant 1891/30 was the most often used Soviet sniper rifle.

Telescopic sight
This sight made the target appear about four times nearer.

Front sight
This sight helped the sniper line up his or her target more accurately.

Trigger
Pulling and releasing this fired the rifle.

Magazine
The ammunition cartridge went here.

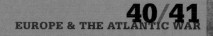

Stalingrad

The Battle of Stalingrad, which began in the summer of 1942, was fought in a ruined city through the freezing winter. The Soviet victory, at the terrible cost of 490,000 Soviet and German lives, marked the first time Hitler's forces had to retreat.

AUG. 23 — Luftwaffe bombs turned much of the city to rubble and killed around 47,000 people. Some women and children were evacuated, but Stalin wanted Stalingrad's civilians to stay and fight.

SEPT. 13 — German troops reached the city center. Snipers were as useful as tanks in combat, because the battle was fought street by street and house by house.

NOV. 19 — 1 million Red Army troops began to encircle and bombard the Germans.

NOV. 23 — 275,000 German soldiers and 50,000 Soviet civilians were trapped for the winter. Vital supplies of food, fuel, and ammunition had to be dropped into the city by plane. Many people died from starvation, frostbite, or disease.

JAN. 1943 — The Soviets captured two key German airfields, preventing the delivery of crucial supplies.

JAN. 31 — The 91,000 Germans still alive surrendered and were taken prisoner. Only 10,000 Soviet civilians survived. These included 904 children, only 9 of whom ever found their parents again.

FEB. 2 — The German prisoners were marched east to Siberia. Tens of thousands died on the journey.

99%

**of Stalingrad's buildings
were destroyed in the siege**

The Holocaust

When the Nazis came to power, more than 9 million Jewish people were living across Europe. In eastern Europe, they spoke Yiddish, and Yiddish culture thrived. Throughout Europe, they were successful in every walk of life. But anti-Semitism was common, and Hitler and the Nazis were able to implement a plan of genocide, or mass murder.

Nazi camps

Starting in 1933, violence toward Jews intensified. The Nazis established concentration camps and forced-labor camps to detain Jews and others considered a danger to the regime. Across Europe, Jews were herded into areas called ghettos, to control them and prepare them for the camps.

Hidden
Some Jewish families—including, famously, the family of Anne Frank—tried to hide. A bookshelf concealed the entrance to the attic where the Frank family hid.

The "Final Solution"

The Final Solution, the plan to exterminate the Jewish people, entered its deadliest phase in 1941. In Russia, more than 1 million Jews were rounded up and murdered. From 1942, extermination camps were used to kill millions of Jewish people from across Europe. Jewish people were herded onto trains in unspeakable conditions and transported to camps to be gassed to death.

Remembering the victims of Nazism

Hundreds of thousands of LGBTQ, Roma, Sinti, and people with disabilities also died at the hands of the Nazis and their collaborators. Soviet prisoners of war were treated with exceptional cruelty, resulting in 3.3 million deaths. An estimated 1.9 million non-Jewish Polish civilians were also killed by the Germans.

A culture disappears
The Jewish population of Europe fell shockingly because of Nazi repression and killings.

Jewish populations in Europe

	Pre–Final Solution population	Killed in Final Solution
Poland	3,300,000	3,000,000
Soviet Union	2,850,000	1,252,000
Hungary	650,000	450,000
Romania	600,000	300,000
Baltic countries	253,000	228,000
Germany and Austria	240,000	210,000

Eyewitness

NAME: Jürgen Stroop

DATE: 1943

LOCATION: Warsaw, Poland

DETAILS: Stroop was a loyal Nazi who joined Hitler's personal guard unit, the Waffen-SS. He held the rank of major general at the time he was sent to Poland, on April 17, 1943, to deal with the Warsaw Ghetto Uprising.

 On April 23 . . . [we were ordered] to complete the combing out of the Warsaw ghetto with the greatest severity and relentless tenacity. I therefore decided to destroy the entire Jewish residential area by setting every block on fire.

Rising up

By spring 1943, with many of their relatives and friends already sent to the death camps, Jewish people in the Warsaw ghetto launched an uprising against the Nazis. But it was a hopeless fight.

Prewar life

This picture shows Jewish children in the city of Lodz, Poland, in 1930. Their parents may have worked in the textile or construction industries. They lived ordinary lives: attending public schools, playing sports, and going to Yiddish theaters. The Lodz Jewish community, numbering more than 230,000, was completely wiped out during the Holocaust.

Remembered

The Nazis and their collaborators killed 1.5 million Jewish children during the Holocaust. In the death camps, children arrived with their relatives, often their whole family. Nearly all those who were under ten years old were killed on arrival. The rest were put to work, often dying from disease or starvation or in random killings. Some of the children's names and the ages at which they died are printed here.

Eyewitness

"Most people who entered through the gates of Auschwitz-Birkenau were confronted with an immediate 'selection'; either to be admitted to the camp or to be killed by gas on arrival."

NAME: Kitty Hart-Moxon

LOCATION: Poland

DETAILS: Born into a Jewish family, Kitty Hart-Moxon survived a ghetto; the massacre of Jews at Belzec, Poland; and prison. In 1943, she was sent to the Auschwitz concentration camp. In 1945, as the Germans retreated, she and hundreds of other women were forcibly marched through Germany and Czechoslovakia. Most died on the journey. She was freed by American soldiers and went to live in England.

❝ Most people who entered through the gates of Auschwitz-Birkenau were confronted with an immediate 'selection'; either to be admitted to the camp or to be killed by gas on arrival. We were marched to be stripped, shaved of all hair, and tattooed on our left forearms. From then on we had no names. I was now number 39934 and my mother, 39933.

There was no water to wash [with] or drink, and no lavatories. The small bread ration was handed out after evening roll call and the camp soup, at midday. It would not sustain life for very long.

For many months I worked in dozens of work groups: loading dead bodies, digging trenches, or working in potato fields, which enabled me to smuggle some potatoes back into the camp.

There was an epidemic of typhus. Most people did not survive when they fell ill, as treatment was nonexistent. But I was taken to my mother, who looked after me and hid me during the daily selections for the gas chambers.

We witnessed the killing of more than half a million people. We girls could not take in what was happening—even though we heard the screams as people were dying. But it sank in eventually when we saw the people disappear before our eyes, never to be seen again, except for the piles of belongings left behind. ❞

"I believe in the Sun,
even when it is not shining.
And I believe in love,
even when there's no one there.
And I believe in God,
even when he is silent.

May there someday be sunshine.
May there someday be happiness.
May there someday be love.
May there someday be peace."

—CARVED ON A WALL BY AN UNKNOWN
VICTIM OF THE HOLOCAUST

Starve Britain

Britain imported huge amounts of food and other vital materials from the United States, Canada, and many other countries. Hitler tried to force an early end to the war by blocking the convoys of cargo ships ferrying these goods across the Atlantic. His weapon was a fleet of U-boats (submarines).

Materials
War uses a lot of resources, and Britain urgently needed these key materials.

Food
During the war, Britain relied heavily on imported foodstuffs (right).

Save everything!
Factories across Britain switched to making planes, tanks, and munitions for the war effort. But materials were in short supply. The government organized salvage drives to collect scrap metal, paper, glass bottles, and rags.

The Land Army
With male farmworkers away at the front, women were drafted to help. By 1944, more than 80,000 "land girls" were planting and harvesting crops.

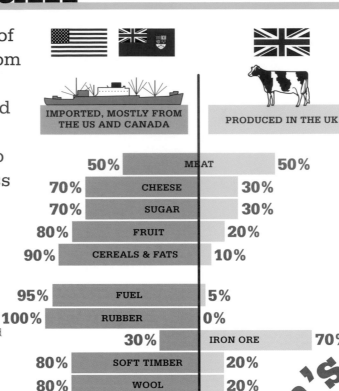

IMPORTED, MOSTLY FROM THE US AND CANADA

PRODUCED IN THE UK

IMPORTED		PRODUCED
50%	MEAT	50%
70%	CHEESE	30%
70%	SUGAR	30%
80%	FRUIT	20%
90%	CEREALS & FATS	10%
95%	FUEL	5%
100%	RUBBER	0%
30%	IRON ORE	70%
80%	SOFT TIMBER	20%
80%	WOOL	20%

Foods people grew during the war:
Cauliflower • Potatoes
Carrots • Turnips
Parsnips • Beets
Runner beans
Leeks

Scarce foods
From January 1940, the British government set limits on how much of certain basic foods people could buy—and the list of foods that were rationed grew as the war went on. Those who could grew their own vegetables in gardens. Cookbooks encouraged making do with dishes such as sheep's head stew.

Foods in extremely short supply:
Bananas • Oranges • Lemons
Fresh peaches • Grapes •
Pineapples • Onions

1 person's ration for

2 OZ. (56.5 G)
CHEESE

1 PT. (568 ML)
MILK

4 OZ. (113 G)
JAM

2 OZ. (56.5 G)
CANDY

Defensive formation

Allied cargo ships traveled in convoys, with escorts of naval ships to fight off submarine attacks. It was desperately important but dangerous work to zigzag across sometimes stormy seas.

An Atlantic convoy

About 45 ships would travel in formation, with 8 protective escorts around them.

5 MILES (8 KM)

1.5 MILES (2.4 KM)

Torpedo attacks

German U-boats torpedoed the convoys. If one ship was hit, the others slowed down to rescue the survivors.

1939
1940
1941
1942
1943
1944
1945

KEY
- US ships built
- Allied ships sunk

0   500   1,000   1,500   2,000   2,500

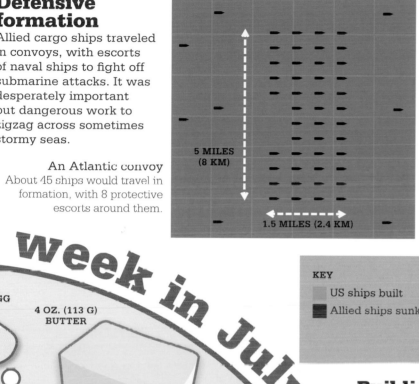

1 week in July 1942

1 EGG

4 OZ. (113 G) BUTTER

2 OZ. (56.5 G) TEA

8 OZ. (226 G) SUGAR

4 OZ. (113 G) HAM

2 OZ. (56.5 G) CHOCOLATE

Building for safety

The number of ships sunk by U-boats reached its peak in 1942, with more than 1,500 lost. But starting in 1943, the tables turned. Intensive US shipbuilding paid off, and larger convoys more successfully countered the German threat.

Nazi rations

Food energy is measured in calories; an adult needs 1,200 calories a day to avoid starvation. In Germany, food was fairly plentiful, but still rationed. In neighboring occupied Poland, supplies were lower, and the Nazis set limits for different groups.

Calorie quotas

Poles were on starvation rations, and Jews faced painful deaths, since they received only 7.5 percent of the nutrition they needed.

2,310
GERMANS

1,790
FOREIGNERS

654
POLES

184
JEWS

U-boat

U-boats were German submarines that attacked Allied merchant vessels crossing the Atlantic. Feared by the Allies, they were also a dangerous place for their crews: More than two-thirds of all U-boat sailors died at sea.

Line of torpedo fire

Supply convoy
Allied ships traveled in convoys (groups) for protection.

Wolf-pack tactics
U-boats hunted in packs, picking off one target at a time.

U-boat

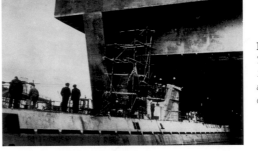

U-boat pens
Many U-boats were based in harbors from France to Norway. Their missions could last weeks or even months.

Dead shot

U-boats (from the German for "undersea boat") spent most of their time on the surface, where they could move faster and visibility was better. When they found a target, they usually attacked at night, under the cover of darkness. They fired underwater missiles called torpedoes.

Conning tower
Two lookouts worked from the tower when the U-boat was on the surface.

Deck gun
The large deck gun could fire 15 cannon rounds a minute and was used to finish off enemy boats.

Net cutter
This cut through enemy antisubmarine nets.

Radio room
Coded messages were sent and received here.

Torpedo tubes
Deadly torpedoes were launched from these.

Spare torpedoes
After these were launched, this space was used for folding beds.

Stern chamber
Flooding this chamber added weight and kept the boat stable.

Bunk beds
The crew slept in shifts, taking turns using the beds.

Toilet
Waste was hand pumped into the sea.

Two periscopes
The front periscope scanned the horizon for ships and planes. The rear one aimed torpedoes.

Rear torpedo tube
This launched missiles from the back of the U-boat.

Twin rudders
These allowed the boat to turn tightly.

Propellers
The propellers drove the U-boat forward or backward.

Hatch
This was closed during dives.

Electric motors
The boat relied on these when underwater.

Diesel engines
On the surface, the boat was powered by two engines.

Galley
Food was prepared on hot plates and in two small ovens.

Batteries
The electric motors ran on rechargeable batteries

Ballast tanks
Distributed around the boat, these tanks were filled or emptied to make the submarine fall or rise.

Control room
The captain and key equipment were based here.

Destroyer escort
Warships like this one were designed to track, chase, and attack submarines.

Type VIIC specifications	
Introduced	1940
Number made	709
Crew members	44
Length	220 ft. (67 m)
Speed on the surface	17 knots (20 mph / 31 kph)
Surface range	8,500 mi. (13,680 km)
Speed underwater	7.6 knots (8.7 mph / 14 kph)
Underwater range	80 mi. (130 km)
Maximum depth	656 ft. (200 m)
Torpedoes	14
Torpedo range	16,500 ft. (5,030 m)

"The only thing that ever really frightened me during the war was the U-boat peril"
—WINSTON CHURCHILL.

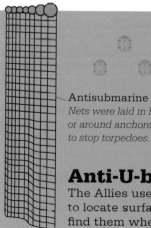
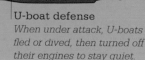

Minefield
Mines were dropped from warships and planes. Magnetic ones were attracted to a U-boat's metal hull.

Depth charges
These were weapons dropped to explode at the estimated depth of a submarine.

Antisubmarine net
Nets were laid in harbors or around anchored ships to stop torpedoes.

Anti-U-boat measures
The Allies used powerful lights or radar to locate surface U-boats, and sonar to find them when they were underwater.

U-boat defense
When under attack, U-boats fled or dived, then turned off their engines to stay quiet.

Codes

Anyone can tune in to radio messages, so important ones were encrypted, or put into a code or cipher. The Allies' ability to break German and Japanese codes and ciphers gave them a vital advantage.

Letter window
This showed the setting of each rotor when the cipher was changed.

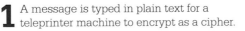

Code
Entire words or phrases are changed to new words, symbols, or letters.

Original (plain text)

Cipher
Each letter is changed. Here, letters have been moved ten places ahead in the alphabet.

daisy
↑
food
↓ ↓ ↓ ↓
p y y n

Cracking Enigma

The Germans invented a cipher machine called Enigma. They changed their ciphers daily and were convinced that they were unbreakable—but they were wrong. Helped by the Polish Cipher Bureau, the British cracked Enigma.

ALAN TURING
Mathematician

Lived: June 23, 1912– June 7, 1954

Famous for: Building the first computer to help crack Enigma

Rotors
These changed each letter as it was typed in.

Bletchley Park
The 2001 film *Enigma* was about Alan Turing and his team at Bletchley Park, England. They first cracked an Enigma message in 1940.

Keyboard
This was where the plain-text message was typed in, one letter at a time.

M 3097

Ticker-tape secrets

Both sides used special teleprinters, which turned text into a cipher and printed it out as a set of punched holes on tape.

1 A message is typed in plain text for a teleprinter machine to encrypt as a cipher.

2 The machine punches holes into ticker tape, which is fed into a special radio transmitter.

3 The receiving teleprinter machine prints out the received encrypted message as punched tape.

4 The message is deciphered using the same cipher settings, so it can be read as plain text.

Enigma
The machine needed two people to work it. One typed the message, one letter at a time. The other read out each new letter that lit up on the lamp board cover, as the plain text became a cipher to be sent.

Lamp board cover
The letters here lit up to show the new encrypted message.

Plug board
Wires here changed some of the letters again, making the cipher even more complicated.

Japanese cipher
William F. Friedman of the US Signals Intelligence Service (SIS) looked for patterns in Japanese coded messages. Thanks to his work, the SIS cracked the Purple cipher in 1940. The Japanese never knew their security was breached.

Wrecked plane
In April 1943, top Japanese admiral Yamamoto Isoroku died after his plane was shot down. The US had deciphered his travel plans.

Dots and dashes
Developed in the 19th century, Morse code represents the letters of the alphabet with sequences of dots and dashes. It was used throughout the war.

MORSE SIGNALING LAMP WITH GREEN AND RED FILTERS

TELEGRAPH KEY FOR SENDING MORSE ELECTRONICALLY

Sending Morse code
Signalers sent messages over long distances in the form of electronic pulses along telegraph wires, and over short distances as flashes of light.

MESSAGE ENCRYPTED, READY TO SEND

MESSAGE RECEIVED, READY TO DECIPHER

War i
Pac

* Who masterminded the
Pearl Harbor attack?

* Where did soldiers battle
knee-deep in mud?

* What was so special
about the B-24?

The Pacific theater

The Japanese captured territory in Southeast Asia, as well as many Pacific islands, before setting up defensive bases across the area. But their failure to knock out the US Navy turned the hope for new territory into a disaster as the US fought back.

YAMAMOTO ISOROKU
Japanese navy

Lived:	1884–1943
Rank in 1941:	Commander of the Combined Fleet

DEC. 1941
Pearl Harbor
Admiral Yamamoto planned Japan's surprise attack on the US Pacific Fleet's base at Pearl Harbor. It was meant to keep the US from interfering with Japanese expansion. Two battleships were sunk and many others damaged with the loss of more than 2,000 American lives.

APR. 1942
No rubber, no tires
Japan's conquests gave it control of Asia's natural rubber, which deprived the United States of this vital material, used for tires and other essential equipment. US scientists developed synthetic rubber from petroleum just before the natural rubber ran out.

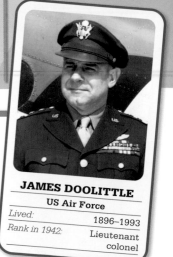

US MILITARY JEEP

FEB. 15, 1942
Japan captured the British colony of Singapore.

AUG. 1942
US troops landed in the Solomon Islands.

•1941   1943

SEPT. 1940
Japan occupied French Indochina and became an ally of Germany and Italy.

JULY 1941
The US and Britain blocked all trade with Japan, and the US stopped supplying Japan with oil.

DEC. 1941
The US declared war on Japan. Germany and Italy declared war on the US.

DEC. 1941
Japan attacked Malaya and the Philippines to control the South China Sea.

APR. 9, 1942
Japan captured the Philippines, preventing US planes from using it as a base.

JUNE 1942
The US won the Battle of Midway, badly damaging the Japanese fleet.

MAR. 1942
Internment
After the Pearl Harbor attack, 110,000 Japanese Americans living across the US were forced to live behind barbed wire, in internment camps. Two-thirds were citizens born in the US. Congress apologized for this in 1988.

JAPANESE AMERICAN CHILDREN

APR. 18, 1942
Doolittle raid
The first US bomb attack on the Japanese capital, Tokyo, was planned and led by veteran pilot James "Jimmy" Doolittle. It did little damage, but this aerial return strike on Japan was a big victory for US morale and propaganda.

JAMES DOOLITTLE
US Air Force

Lived:	1896–1993
Rank in 1942:	Lieutenant colonel

MAY 1942
Battle of the Coral Sea

US ships intercepted a Japanese fleet aiming to invade New Guinea and the Solomon Islands. For four days, each side sent planes to drop bombs and torpedoes. There was no outright winner, but Japan's losses were greater.

USS *LEXINGTON*, SINKING IN THE CORAL SEA

OCT. 23–26, 1944
Leyte Gulf

A series of massive battles was fought in the waters of Leyte Gulf, near the Philippines. The US victory cut off the supply route from mainland Japan to its forces in Southeast Asia, a plan masterminded by Admiral Nimitz.

CHESTER NIMITZ
US Navy

Lived:	1885–1966
Rank in 1944:	Commander in chief of the Pacific Fleet

JAN. 1943
At the Casablanca Conference, Churchill and Roosevelt agreed that they should insist on unconditional surrender from the Axis powers.

NOV. 1943
US landings on Bougainville, in the Solomon Islands, isolated Japanese forces and destroyed some of their key bases.

JUNE 19–20, 1944
Japan lost 3 carriers and 426 of its 473 operational aircraft in the Battle of the Philippine Sea.

Dots represent yearly increases.

APR. 12, 1945
President Roosevelt died and was replaced by his vice president, Harry S. Truman.

•1944 •1945

MAR. 1945
A US air raid set Tokyo on fire. At least 80,000 people died, and 1.5 million lost their homes. US troops also captured Iwo Jima.

FEB. 1943
War production

The US economy was set up for war. Car factories switched to building military vehicles. Millions of women joined the workforce, recruited by the newly created War Manpower Commission.

A RIVETER AT WORK ON A BOMBER IN A TEXAS FACTORY

APR. 1944
Battle of Imphal-Kohima

Battles at Imphal and Kohima, in India, turned back the Japanese invasion of Southeast Asia. Now Allied planes could fly from the area to attack the Japanese, who began to retreat through Burma.

CLEARING THE ROAD BETWEEN IMPHAL AND KOHIMA OF JAPANESE SOLDIERS

nearly 300,000:
the number of military aircraft built in the United States during the war

Pearl Harbor

On December 7, 1941, the Japanese attacked Pearl Harbor, on the Hawaiian island of Oahu. They hoped to wipe out the US Pacific Fleet, most of which was docked there. The surprise attack brought the United States into the war.

6:10 AM — 183 planes took off from 6 Japanese aircraft carriers in the ocean 230 miles (370 km) north of the target. There were 51 dive-bombers, 49 bombers, 40 torpedo bombers, and 43 fighters.

JAPANESE SAILORS WAVING OFF THEIR PLANES

7:45 AM — Dive-bombers attacked local airfields to give the Japanese control of the air. In all, 188 US planes were destroyed.

7:53 AM — The Japanese aimed bombs and torpedoes at the 8 battleships anchored in the harbor.

8:10 AM — The USS *Arizona* was hit by a bomb that ignited the gunpowder in its hold (cargo deck). In the ensuing explosion, 1,177 men died.

8:54 AM — A second wave of 78 dive-bombers, 54 bombers, and 35 fighters arrived to attack the other 76 ships in the harbor, plus oil tanks and docks.

9:55 AM — The second-wave planes returned to their carriers. They left behind 19 badly damaged or sunk ships—and a shocked nation. Comparatively few Japanese planes—29—were lost in the attack.

2,403

Americans were killed in the attack on Pearl Harbor

Culture during wartime

Both at home and on the front line, wartime music, radio shows, and movies expressed what people were fighting for and how much they missed their loved ones. People could escape their troubles for a while when they listened to a comedy on the radio or danced to the latest popular songs. Media had a more serious side, too, as governments everywhere used it to persuade citizens that their cause was right.

Hollywood's leading role

Eager to forget the hardships of war, people flocked to movie theaters to watch musicals and comedies. Hollywood helped the US government by producing films in which heroes fought evil invaders; the villains were nearly always German, Italian, or Japanese. Female characters in films were often shown doing their part as nurses or spies.

Persuasion

Governments used propaganda (see page 17) at home to explain the war and encourage support for it. They also created propaganda to use against their enemies. Both sides tried to destroy their opponents' morale with radio broadcasts for enemy troops. An Allied tactic was to drop propaganda leaflets into occupied territory.

GIVE 'EM BOTH BARRELS

ENCOURAGING PEOPLE TO WORK AND FIGHT

Screen support

Like many movies of the time, *Casablanca* (1942) depicts Nazis as arrogant and members of the resistance as brave. It portrays the US as a haven for the oppressed.

BUY WAR BONDS

RAISING MONEY FOR THE WAR EFFORT

We Can Do It!

BUILDING A SENSE OF NATIONAL IDENTITY

HE'S WATCHING YOU

SHOWING THE ENEMY AS EVIL

Humphrey BOGART · Ingrid BERGMAN · Paul HENREID

A HAL B. WALLIS PRODUCTION

"*Casablanca*"

CLAUDE RAINS · CONRAD VEIDT · SYDNEY GREENSTREET · PETER LORRE
Directed by MICHAEL CURTIZ

All that jazz

Radio was how most people heard music, and it helped popularize jazz and swing. Hitler tried to ban jazz because of its links with Black Americans and Jews, but many German troops listened to it.

Super sounds

"Big band" groups performed jazz and swing on the radio and in dance halls. Pianist Duke Ellington's band was one of the most popular.

Boosting morale

The United Service Organizations (USO) put on up to 700 shows a day to keep up the spirits of US servicemen and women around the world. Stars of USO "camp shows" ranged from Laurel and Hardy to Lucille Ball. German troops had "front theater" plays and cabarets.

Zarah Leander

Deep-voiced Swedish singer Zarah Leander was a superstar in Germany. She fled the country after her home was bombed in 1944.

Hope for all

Comedian Bob Hope was a huge attraction for the troops. In summer 1944, he island-hopped across the South Pacific to perform more than 150 shows, many of which were broadcast on live radio.

Women and the war

These assembly-line workers are completing a B-17 bomber. During the war, the United States' female workforce rose from 12 to 18 million; there were similar increases in other fighting countries. Women took on everything from working on farms and driving buses and trains to operating radar, spying, and, of course, fighting. From 1945, millions of *Trümmerfrauen* ("rubble women") cleared Germany's wrecked cities brick by brick.

Wartime childhood

War destroyed childhoods, as youngsters dealt with the losses of fathers, mothers, and homes. Everywhere, children struggled with shortages of food, clothes, and toys. Millions fled from battle zones or occupying armies. And millions more were killed by terrible bombings and in the Holocaust (see pages 42–45).

Japan

Bombings and food shortages forced many Japanese families to move from the cities to the countryside. The most nimble-fingered girls worked in factories, making fire balloons—bomb-carrying hydrogen balloons that were launched toward the United States and Canada.

Germany

In Germany, children aged 10–18 were expected to join Nazi youth organizations. Girls cared for the wounded in hospitals. Boys in the Hitler Youth were trained to help during air raids. They operated searchlights, fired antiaircraft guns, and participated in the cleanup.

Eyewitness

NAME: Emmy Werner

DATE: Born in 1929

FROM: Near Frankfurt, Germany

DETAILS: Emmy Werner was 10 when her country went to war. She later moved to the United States and became a psychologist.

❝ I was 12 . . . and volunteered for the . . . air-raid watch. . . . We became experts at spotting incendiaries that had penetrated the roof of our schoolhouse or the classroom ceilings. Armed with buckets, we would race to throw sand over the eight-sided metal sticks before they exploded. **❞**

Antiaircraft gun
From January 1943, boys in the Hitler Youth worked German antiaircraft guns.

Eyewitness

NAME: Shizue Kobayashi

DATE: Born in 1934

FROM: Saitama-ken, Japan

DETAILS: Shizue Kobayashi lived in Japan until she was 22 years old. In 1956, she immigrated to the United States to marry an airman who used to play baseball with the children at an orphanage she visited.

❝ I wasn't allowed to eat as much as I wanted, just enough to keep me alive. After our potatoes were gone, we ate weeds we found in the yard. We were lucky, though, because a lot of people were dying of hunger. **❞**

Eyewitness

NAME: Joan Dooley

DATE: 1942

FROM: Wichita, KS

DETAILS: Joan Dooley was a 12-year-old Girl Scout when she wrote to General Douglas MacArthur, supreme commander of the southwest Pacific war.

❝ My mother saves grease for bullets. I also buy a war stamp every time I get a quarter. We save paper, all kinds of metal and rubber. I have a bicycle but I don't very often ride it to save rubber tires. . . . We Girl Scouts are doing our bit by taking care of small children so that the parents may work in war factories.**❞**

United States

American children helped the war effort by collecting newspapers, rubber tires, and tin cans for recycling. In the month of October 1942, 30 million children collected 1.5 million tons of scrap metal for producing aircraft and munitions.

Britain

In Britain, hundreds of thousands of children were evacuated from bomb-threatened cities to the safer but unfamiliar countryside. Candy was rationed, along with other foods, and any treats were highly prized. Children swapped old toys and books and wished for new, war-themed books about tanks, battleships, or warplanes.

Eyewitness

NAME: Jean Bruce

DATE: Born in 1935

FROM: Manchester, Britain

DETAILS: Jean Bruce was 3 years old when the war started, but she remembers the air raids, rationing, and her Mickey Mouse gas mask. She later immigrated to Canada.

❝ People had to queue up for everything (though rationing made things fairer). Sometimes Mum would see a queue forming and join it, not even knowing what was for sale at that shop. One orange was a very rare treat carefully shared out segment by segment, and I didn't have a banana throughout the war. **❞**

War bonds
Even children were encouraged to buy war bonds, which raised money for the war effort.

Ruined Berlin
For children in cities across Europe, the daily walk to school became a trek across a bomb site.

A night out
To escape air raids, families crammed into cold, damp shelters (like this reconstruction) in their yards.

Sea battles

By early 1942, Japan was victorious throughout the Pacific and Southeast Asia, so it needed to defend the supply routes to these conquests against attacks by the Allied fleet. The Pacific became a war zone, where submarines, warships, and aircraft carriers battled.

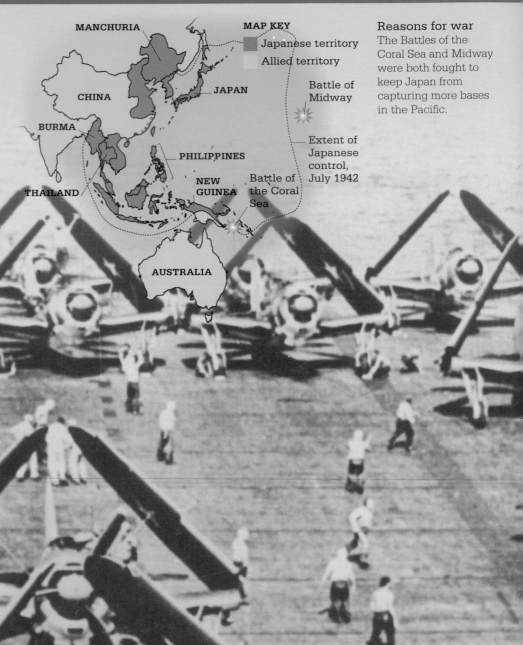

Reasons for war
The Battles of the Coral Sea and Midway were both fought to keep Japan from capturing more bases in the Pacific.

MANCHURIA

MAP KEY
Japanese territory
Allied territory

CHINA

JAPAN

BURMA

Battle of Midway

PHILIPPINES

Extent of Japanese control, July 1942

THAILAND

NEW GUINEA

Battle of the Coral Sea

AUSTRALIA

Battle of the Coral Sea: losses		
	US	Japan
Aircraft carriers	1	1
Warships	1	4
Oil tankers	1	0
Aircraft	66	77
Men	654	1,074

Battle of the Coral Sea

In May 1942, Japan and the US engaged in a battle in the Coral Sea. The ships involved never saw or fired on one another. Instead, each side used an aircraft carrier to launch bombers to attack the enemy fleet. After four days, the result was a costly draw.

Doomed aircraft carrier
Curtiss SBC Helldiver two-seat scout bombers and dive bombers prepare for take off from the flight deck of an aircraft carrier of the US Navy on December 1, 1943, off the Philippines.

Battle of Midway

Japan planned to draw out the US fleet with a decoy attack on the Aleutian Islands. On June 4, 1942, one force would ambush the US carriers off Midway Island while another conquered Midway itself. However, the US had cracked Japan's coded messages. It hit the Japanese with waves of torpedoes and dive-bombers. Midway was a turning point in the Pacific war. Japan never recovered from its losses.

Battle of Midway: losses

	US	Japan
Aircraft carriers	1	4
Warships	1	1
Aircraft	132	275
Men	307	3,507

1 Aleutian attack
The decoy strike was to allow Admiral Nagumo to destroy the US fleets while Admiral Yamamoto conquered Midway.

2 Early draw
The first waves of Japanese and US planes set off at almost the same time. Neither side managed to deliver a knockout blow to its target.

3 US success
While the Japanese fought off one wave of US attackers, another US group got through and hit three carriers.

Backup
Planes from USS Hornet headed to protect Midway Island.

4 Massive defeat
Hiryu launched planes at USS *Yorktown* before it sank. Admiral Yamamoto's approaching fleet had to retreat.

MAP KEY
- US Task Force 17
- US Task Force 16
- Japanese fleets

JAPAN

ALEUTIAN ISLANDS

Admiral Nagumo's fleet
Admiral Yamamoto's fleet

MIDWAY

Task Force 17 *(including USS Yorktown)*

Japan's planned attack routes

Area under US submarine surveillance

Task Force 16 *(including USS Enterprise and Hornet)*

HAWAIIAN ISLANDS

180° W **179° W** **178° W** **177° W**

Nagumo's fleet of four carriers
Soryu
Akagi
Hiryu
Kaga

7 AM
Bombers took off from US carriers

USS *Enterprise*
USS *Hornet*

47 of the 51 US torpedo planes shot down

USS *Yorktown*

4:30 AM
Japanese bombers took off to attack Midway.

4:45–6:00 AM
US bombers took off from Midway Island

30° N

Hit
Akagi, Soryu, and Kaga sank

11 AM
Dive-bombers were launched from Hiryu.

12 PM
USS Yorktown was hit.

8:30 AM
All three US carriers launched planes to attack Nagumo's fleet.

June 5
Hiryu sank.

5:05 PM
Hiryu *was severely hit.*

1:30 PM
Torpedo bombers were launched from Hiryu.

3:30 PM
USS Enterprise launched dive-bombers to attack Hiryu.

2:40 PM
USS Yorktown was badly hit.

Jungle fighting

From December 1941, Japan invaded many Pacific islands, as well as Asian countries such as Malaya and Burma. It quickly learned how to fight in the dense jungle. Now US, British, Australian, and other Allied troops had to do the same. This fighting was up close and nasty, as small groups crawled on their bellies or waded through swamps.

Under attack

Enemies could be lurking above- or belowground—but they were only one of the dangers soldiers faced in the jungle. Troops on both sides feared mosquito bites, which could transmit deadly malaria or dengue fever.

Jungle worries
For every 1 combat casualty, Allied doctors treated as many as 100 soldiers suffering from heatstroke or tropical diseases.

Extreme heat
Temperatures could soar to 100°F (38°C), causing exhaustion and dehydration.

Bad water
Microorganisms in dirty water led to dysentery, cholera, and typhoid.

Venomous snakes
Vipers could kill with a single bite.

Malaria
This disease caused fever, convulsions, and death.

Dengue fever
This virus led to fever, rashes, and even death.

Tall grass
Razor-sharp kunai grass cut through flesh like a knife.

Jungle rot
Tropical ulcers formed on the skin and rotted away the flesh.

Leeches
These bloodsuckers left wounds that could soon become infected.

Eyewitness

NAME: George Henry Johnston

DATE: 1942

FROM: Melbourne, Australia

DETAILS: Johnston (1912–70) was a war correspondent for the *Melbourne Argus* newspaper.

❝ Churned up by the troops of both armies, the track itself is now knee-deep in thick black mud. For the last ten days no man's clothing has been dry, and all have slept when sleep was possible in pouring rain under sodden blankets. Each man carries his personal equipment, firearms, ammunition supply, and five days' rations. Every hour is a nightmare. ❞

Mud march
In November 1943, US marines headed to Bougainville Island, part of New Guinea, to confront the Japanese.

80%
of US soldiers in some South Pacific units were infected with **malaria**

Japanese tactics

Japanese snipers lashed themselves to trees or hid in dugouts in order to surprise the enemy, particularly at night. They would call out in English to trick Allies in the dark, and they always fought to the death.

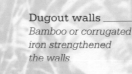

Dugout
The main bunker could house a small detachment of troops.

Crawl trench
These tunnels connected the dugout to the foxholes.

Foxhole
One-man gun pits radiated out from the main dugout.

Dugout walls
Bamboo or corrugated iron strengthened the walls

Fire!
The sniper or machine gunner fired through a slit in the wall.

Camouflage
Earth, brushwood, or leaves hid the whole complex from sight

Hideout
Both sides used dugouts like this one to rest in between patrols or as bases for surprise sniper attacks.

Holdouts

Japanese troops were trained not to give up. Some, left behind in remote areas, never heard that the war was over. These soldiers stayed in their jungle dugouts for years, or even decades, because no one had ordered them to leave.

Holdout Hiroo Onoda surrenders
Officer Hiroo Onoda was 52 when he handed over his sword, dagger, rifle, and hand grenades in 1974. He had hidden in the Philippines for nearly 30 years.

Guns

During the war, gun technology improved. At first, soldiers put up with outdated models. Later, they were armed with new, state-of-the-art weapons that had faster firing rates and greater accuracy, and were less likely to jam or overheat.

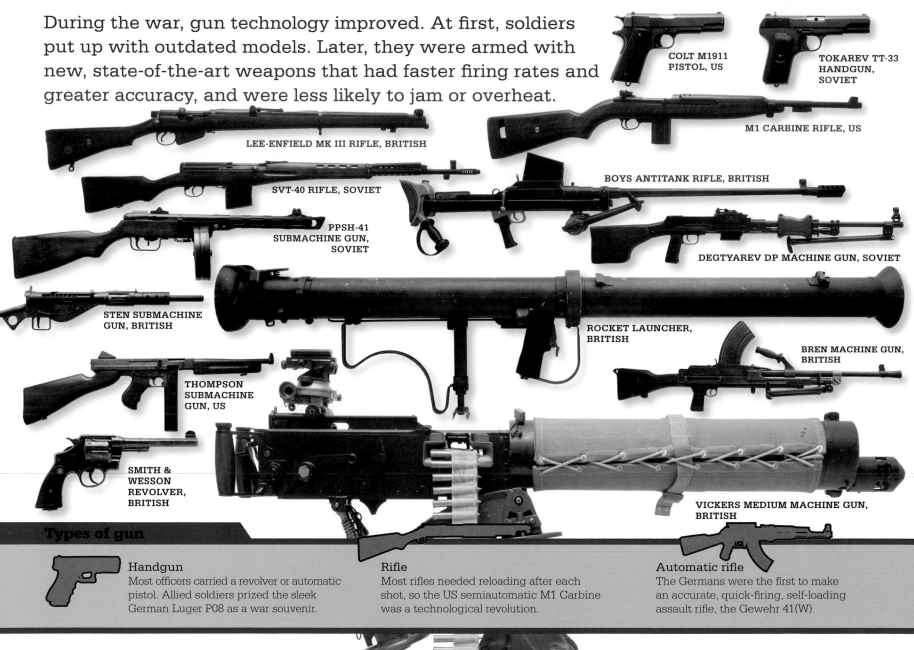

COLT M1911 PISTOL, US

TOKAREV TT-33 HANDGUN, SOVIET

M1 CARBINE RIFLE, US

LEE-ENFIELD MK III RIFLE, BRITISH

SVT-40 RIFLE, SOVIET

BOYS ANTITANK RIFLE, BRITISH

PPSH-41 SUBMACHINE GUN, SOVIET

DEGTYAREV DP MACHINE GUN, SOVIET

STEN SUBMACHINE GUN, BRITISH

ROCKET LAUNCHER, BRITISH

BREN MACHINE GUN, BRITISH

THOMPSON SUBMACHINE GUN, US

SMITH & WESSON REVOLVER, BRITISH

VICKERS MEDIUM MACHINE GUN, BRITISH

Types of gun

Handgun
Most officers carried a revolver or automatic pistol. Allied soldiers prized the sleek German Luger P08 as a war souvenir.

Rifle
Most rifles needed reloading after each shot, so the US semiautomatic M1 Carbine was a technological revolution.

Automatic rifle
The Germans were the first to make an accurate, quick-firing, self-loading assault rifle, the Gewehr 41(W).

CARCANO M91 RIFLE, ITALIAN

TYPE 38 RIFLE, JAPANESE

BERETTA MODEL 38 SUBMACHINE GUN, ITALIAN

TYPE 99 MACHINE GUN, JAPANESE

STG44 (ALSO KNOWN AS MP43 AND MP44) AUTOMATIC RIFLE, GERMAN

MG42 MACHINE GUN, GERMAN

MP40 SUBMACHINE GUN, GERMAN

BROWNING HI POWER HANDGUN, GERMAN

MAUSER KAR98K RIFLE, GERMAN

MAUSER C96 HANDGUN, GERMAN

PZB 39 ANTITANK RIFLE, GERMAN

LUGER P08 HANDGUN, GERMAN

TYPE 14 PISTOL, JAPANESE

Submachine gun
These shot 400 to 800 rounds per minute in short bursts. Top performers were the German MP40 and the US Thompson.

Machine gun
Each section of eight to ten men had support from a lightweight machine gun. Heavy machine guns, mounted on tripods, were better for long-range targets.

Antitank weapon
In 1942, the US Army invented the rocket-firing bazooka, a weapon that can penetrate thick tank armor.

POWs

All sides held POWs, or prisoners of war—captured military personnel—in camps to prevent them from fighting again. In countries that had signed the Geneva Conventions, such as Britain and the United States, POWs were mostly treated well. In the Soviet Union and Japan, they were starved and beaten.

Field work
POWs in Britain could not escape their island prison, and many were trusted to work on farms.

Camps in the West

POW camps were set up all over Europe and the United States. Prisoners occupied themselves with craftwork, reading, and learning new skills. Sometimes they worked on local farms or built roads and waterways. For most, it was a boring but safe wait for the war to end.

Eyewitness

NAME: Janina Skrzynska

POW: Dec. 1944–Apr. 1945

FROM: Poland

DETAILS: Skrzynska was in the Polish Home Army; she was captured by the Nazis after the Warsaw Uprising. She was held in a women's camp at Oberlangen, Germany.

❝ One barrack was used as a chapel, while two more were left empty. These we exploited as an extra supply of fuel: We took out planks from the bunks, pulled up floorboards. . . . In the mornings and evenings [we had] a tepid herbal tea, . . . moldy bread, the occasional piece of margarine, or a spoonful of beetroot marmalade. At midday, . . . soup from bitter cabbage or grubby peas with two or three jacket potatoes. **❞**

Changi prisoners
Changi was a notoriously tough Japanese POW camp in Singapore, where inmates had a simple choice— work or starve.

Colditz Castle
This fortress near Dresden, Germany, was for POWs whose escapes had failed. The war ended before they could fly the glider they had built in the attic!

Great escapes

Allied POWs in Germany made many escape attempts. Their efforts ranged from making fake guard uniforms and simply walking out, to digging tunnels to get beyond the fences. Of the 76 who tried this one night from Stalag Luft III, 3 made it back to Britain, 23 were returned to the camp, and 50 were shot on Hitler's orders.

Camps in the East

Life for prisoners in Japanese POW camps was extremely harsh. POWs were fed tiny amounts of rice. Beatings were common, and POWs were forced to work in mines or on a railroad between Burma and Thailand.

60,000

Allied POWs were forced to help build the Burma Railway; one in five died

March of death

In April 1942, the Japanese marched captured soldiers 85 miles (135 km) in six days to a camp. They beat or killed those who fell—10,000 Filipinos and 650 Americans died.

International parcels

Some fortunate POWs received Red Cross packages containing treats such as butter, cookies, chocolate, and dried food

B-24

More B-24 Liberators were built than any other US military plane. This long-range bomber flew faster and farther than other planes, and with heavier loads. But it burned quickly if its fuel tanks were hit, so it was nicknamed the "flying coffin."

All-arounder

The B-24 was far more than just a heavy bomber. It could attack submarines and ships, lay mines, transport people and supplies, and carry out photographic reconnaissance missions and weather checks.

Building B-24s
Ford's Willow Run plant, near Detroit, MI, was built for making B-24s. The assembly line was 1 mile (1.6 km) long.

Oxygen bottles
Spare oxygen was for the crew to breathe.

Top gun turret
The plane's engineer manned the gun in this Plexiglas turret.

Cockpit crew
B-24 pilots needed strength to handle the heavy controls.

Nose turret
This protective turret had a shield of bulletproof Plexiglas.

Bomb bay doors
The doors rolled back into the fuselage to keep the plane streamlined.

B-24 specifications

Introduced	1941
Number made	18,482
Crew members	8-10
Length	67 ft. 8 in. (20.6 m)
Weight (empty)	36,500 lb. (116,556 kg)
Wingspan	110 ft (33.5 m)
Range	2,100 mi. (3,380 km)
Guns	10 machine guns (sometimes 11)
Bomb cargo (short range)	8,000 lb. (3,600 kg)
Bomb cargo (long range)	5,000 lb. (2,300 kg)

Machine guns
These .50-caliber guns could fire 800 rounds a minute.

Electric heaters
Heaters kept the guns from freezing in the cold, high air.

Nose wheel
This prevented the plane from tipping when on the ground.

Bombs away!
Most B-24s carried ten 500 lb. (227 kg) bombs, or five 1,000 lb. (454 kg) ones.

18 hours: the time taken to build each B-24 Liberator

Tail gun turret
This could swing 180 degrees for fast fighting.

Camera mount
This held the camera used for reconnaissance.

Fuselage
The flat-sided, boxy fuselage allowed maximum cargo space.

Stabilizer
Twin tails helped keep the plane more stable while in the air.

Waist gun position
Gunners working in the waist (another name for the fuselage) also released tinfoil, called chaff, to confuse enemy radar.

Ball turret
This gun turret could turn in a full circle. It tucked into the fuselage during landings and takeoffs.

Turbocharged
Four air-cooled, 1,200-horsepower engines powered the B-24.

Bomb types

The versatile B-24 carried crater-making general-purpose bombs and fire-starting cluster bombs. Other missiles included radio-guided ones for tricky targets, and torpedoes for dropping in water.

GENERAL-PURPOSE BOMB
AN-M64: 500 LB. (227 KG)

INCENDIARY CLUSTER BOMB
AN-M17A1: 500 LB. (227 KG)

RADIO-GUIDED BOMB
VB-1 AZON: 1,000 LB. (454 KG)

Retractable wheel
The two main wheels used on the ground folded into the wings during flight.

Davis wing
Clever shaping enabled the wings to lift the plane with its heavy loads.

Island-hopping

Jungle warfare through Southeast Asia was slow and deadly. The Allies needed a different strategy against the Japanese. From June 1943, they began to conquer islands around powerful Japanese bases. As the Allies gained control of sea and air, they were able to keep supplies from reaching enemy troops. This leapfrogging to the next target en route to Japan itself was called island-hopping.

Kamikaze killers

The Japanese adopted a terrifying new tactic in October 1944 at the Battle of Leyte Gulf—kamikaze, or "divine wind," attacks. Pilots flew bomb-filled planes straight into targets. By the end of the war, the Japanese had carried out about 2,800 of these suicide missions.

In for the kill
A kamikaze fighter plane hurtles toward the USS *Missouri*, off Okinawa, in April 1945. The battleship survived the attack.

4 **End of the line**
The advancing Allied lines met at Okinawa, which became their base for air attacks on Japan.

3 **Leyte Gulf**
In October 1944, Japan counterattacked in the Battle of Leyte Gulf. Much of its fleet was destroyed.

MANCHURIA

KOREA

Sea of Japan

JAPAN

East China Sea

CHINA

Okinawa
June 1945

Iwo Jima
Feb.–Mar. 1945

BURMA

South China Sea

PHILIPPINES

Philippine Sea
June 1944

Leyte Gulf
Oct. 1944

PALAU ISLANDS

Peleliu
Sept.–Nov. 1944

Mindanao

Morotai
Sept. 1944

DUTCH BORNEO

NEW GUINEA

Banda Sea

JAVA

Timor Sea

AUSTRALIA

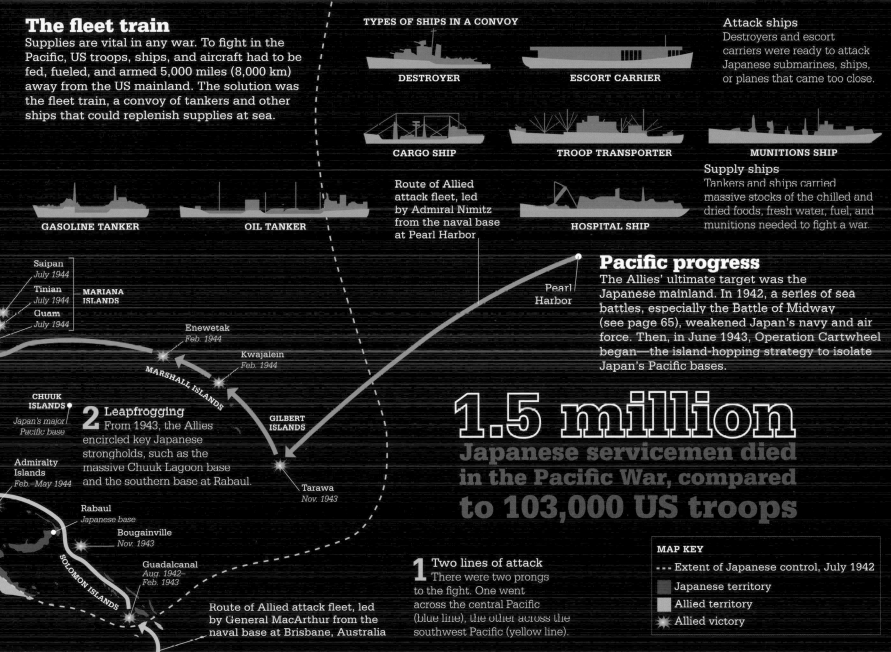

The fleet train

Supplies are vital in any war. To fight in the Pacific, US troops, ships, and aircraft had to be fed, fueled, and armed 5,000 miles (8,000 km) away from the US mainland. The solution was the fleet train, a convoy of tankers and other ships that could replenish supplies at sea.

TYPES OF SHIPS IN A CONVOY

DESTROYER

ESCORT CARRIER

CARGO SHIP

TROOP TRANSPORTER

MUNITIONS SHIP

GASOLINE TANKER

OIL TANKER

HOSPITAL SHIP

Attack ships
Destroyers and escort carriers were ready to attack Japanese submarines, ships, or planes that came too close.

Supply ships
Tankers and ships carried massive stocks of the chilled and dried foods, fresh water, fuel, and munitions needed to fight a war.

Route of Allied attack fleet, led by Admiral Nimitz from the naval base at Pearl Harbor

Pacific progress
The Allies' ultimate target was the Japanese mainland. In 1942, a series of sea battles, especially the Battle of Midway (see page 65), weakened Japan's navy and air force. Then, in June 1943, Operation Cartwheel began—the island-hopping strategy to isolate Japan's Pacific bases.

Saipan
July 1944

Tinian
July 1944

MARIANA ISLANDS

Guam
July 1944

Enewetak
Feb. 1944

Kwajalein
Feb. 1944

MARSHALL ISLANDS

GILBERT ISLANDS

Pearl Harbor

CHUUK ISLANDS
Japan's major Pacific base

2 Leapfrogging
From 1943, the Allies encircled key Japanese strongholds, such as the massive Chuuk Lagoon base and the southern base at Rabaul.

Admiralty Islands
Feb.–May 1944

Tarawa
Nov. 1943

1.5 million
Japanese servicemen died in the Pacific War, compared to 103,000 US troops

Rabaul
Japanese base

Bougainville
Nov. 1943

SOLOMON ISLANDS

Guadalcanal
Aug. 1942–Feb. 1943

Route of Allied attack fleet, led by General MacArthur from the naval base at Brisbane, Australia

1 Two lines of attack
There were two prongs to the fight. One went across the central Pacific (blue line), the other across the southwest Pacific (yellow line).

MAP KEY

- - - Extent of Japanese control, July 1942

■ Japanese territory

■ Allied territory

✳ Allied victory

The Battle of Iwo Jima

Iwo Jima is a tiny Pacific island 700 miles (1,100 km) from Japan's capital, Tokyo. Allied planes needed to use its airstrips for attacks on the Japanese mainland. It was a key target.

Japanese defenders on Iwo Jima dug bunkers connected by miles of tunnels and hid artillery positions. On February 19, 1945, 30,000 US marines began to land on the beaches. When the fierce fighting ended five weeks later, most of the roughly 20,000 Japanese troops were dead; 6,800 Americans were killed. The Japanese had proven again they would fight to the end. This greatly influenced the US's decision to drop atomic bombs on Japan so devastating they would end the war.

War in A
& the Mid

* Which German general was known as the Desert Fox?

* What dangers did tank commanders face?

* How did the Allies win their victory at El Alamein?

frica
dle East

Africa and the Middle East

For 32 months, starting from September 1940, Allied and Axis forces battled back and forth in North and East Africa. This was a deadly game of chess played across the hot desert with tanks, artillery, and troops. The prize was access to Middle Eastern oil.

APR. 1941
The siege of Tobruk
Rommel's forces surrounded and bombarded Tobruk, trapping 14,000 Australians. Fighting back from a defensive network of trenches and tunnels, the Australian troops nicknamed themselves "the rats of Tobruk."

GERMAN TROOPS AND TANKS NEAR TOBRUK

JULY 1940
Naval attack
The British wanted to keep the Germans from taking control of the French fleet in the Algerian port of Mers El Kébir. They attacked, sinking three battleships.

JAN. 1941
Allied forces swept on from Egypt to take the key port of Tobruk, in Libya.

DEC. 1941
The Allies forced Rommel's army away from Tobruk to relieve the siege.

1941 **1942**

Dots represent yearly increases.

JUNE 10, 1940
Italy declared war on Britain and France. Mussolini had 300,000 Italian and African troops based in Libya.

JULY 1940
In East Africa, Italy attacked the British colonies of Sudan and Kenya.

DEC. 1940
British troops, numbering 36,000, defeated a force of 75,000 Italians in Egypt.

NOV. 27, 1941
Italian forces lost a key battle at Gondar, Abyssinia (now Ethiopia), with the surrender of 23,500 men. Italy was finally forced out of East Africa.

22,195
gallons (85,000 L): the amount of fuel the Afrika Korps needed every week

ERWIN ROMMEL
German army

In Africa:	Feb. 1941–May 1943
Rank in 1941:	General
Nickname:	The Desert Fox

FEB. 1941
The Afrika Korps
German forces, battle hardened from their successes in Europe, arrived to support the struggling Italians. The German Afrika Korps was led by Rommel, an experienced and clever general.

JULY 1–27, 1942
First Battle of El Alamein

The small Egyptian town was the last line of Allied defense before the Suez Canal. Allies and Germans battled to a draw that weakened Rommel's overextended army.

A BRITISH 5.5-INCH (14 CM) ARTILLERY GUN USED AT EL ALAMEIN

JULY 10, 1943
Invasion of Sicily

It took a total of 450,000 Allied soldiers 38 days to drive retreating Italian and German troops from the island of Sicily in the Mediterranean Sea. For this mission, code-named Operation Husky, Allied troops arrived by boat and by parachute.

BRITISH TROOPS LANDING ON SICILY

JAN. 1943
The British took Tripoli, in Libya, forcing the Axis armies back east into Tunisia.

NOV. 1942
To the east, in Operation Torch, the Allies landed in French North Africa.

SEPT. 8, 1943
Italy surrendered. Allied troops had invaded five days earlier, and they kept advancing from the south.

• 1943 • **1944 •**

MAY 1942
Rommel's attack at Gazala, Libya, pushed the Allies back into Egypt.

JUNE 21, 1942
The German Afrika Korps captured Tobruk and 35,000 Allied troops.

AUG. 1942
The first of 300 US Sherman tanks arrived in North Africa. They were to prove vital.

FEB. 19–25, 1943
The Battle of Kasserine Pass was Rommel's last victory, as his forces beat the newly arrived US troops.

MAY 1943
With hardly any supplies left, Axis forces surrendered in Tunisia.

OCT. 13, 1943
Italy switched sides and declared war on Germany, its former ally.

BERNARD MONTGOMERY
British army

In Africa:	Aug. 1942 – May 1943
Rank in 1942:	General
Nickname:	Monty

AUG. 1942
Troop morale

General Bernard Montgomery took command of the British Eighth Army. He made speeches directly to his troops, explaining how he planned to defeat Rommel. This made him very popular.

OCT. 23–NOV. 4, 1942
Second Battle of El Alamein

Montgomery used rubber tanks, wooden trucks, and dummy railroads to deceive the Germans. His victory at El Alamein marked the point at which Rommel began his retreat.

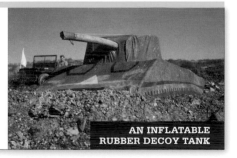

AN INFLATABLE RUBBER DECOY TANK

War in the desert

War came to North Africa in September 1940, when Italy used its African colony Libya as the base for an advance on British-occupied Egypt. Mussolini's ultimate target was the crucial Suez Canal. When the Allies pushed the Italians back, Hitler sent his Afrika Korps to the fight. Now the desert war raged.

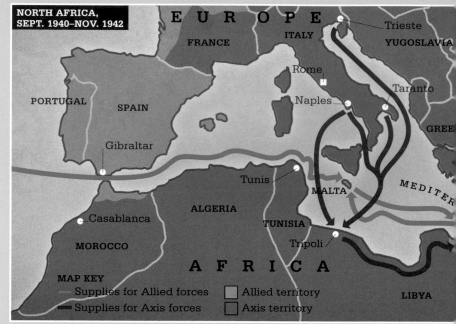

NORTH AFRICA, SEPT. 1940–NOV. 1942

EUROPE
FRANCE
ITALY
Trieste
YUGOSLAVIA
PORTUGAL
SPAIN
Rome
Taranto
Naples
Gibraltar
GREE
Tunis
MALTA
MEDITER
ALGERIA
Casablanca
TUNISIA
MOROCCO
Tripoli
AFRICA
LIBYA

MAP KEY
— Supplies for Allied forces ☐ Allied territory
— Supplies for Axis forces ☐ Axis territory

Minefields
Millions of mines were hidden just below the sand, primed to blow up if tanks drove over them.

Desert tactics
Both sides often began attacks with blasts of artillery; then the infantry would advance, supported by tanks. It was important to stay within reach of supplies, or fuel-hungry tanks might be stranded. Spies provided intelligence about where the other side was and where it was going.

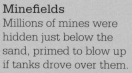

Moving at night
Troop movements across the open desert took place at night, under cover of darkness.

Decoy tanks
Tanks dragged metal chains to create clouds of dust that looked like an army on the move.

Poisoning water
If troops retreated, they poisoned water supplies to keep this vital resource from the enemy.

Supply routes
Resources were scarce in this undeveloped territory, much of which was desert, so both sides had to bring all their supplies. Tobruk was a major prize because it was the port nearest to the front lines, where the armies needed food, fuel, and ammunition in vast quantities.

Fighting team
Hitler created his Afrika Korps in February 1941, selecting his popular commander Erwin Rommel to lead it. Rommel used the Wehrmacht's fast, surprise blitzkrieg methods (see pages 22–23) brilliantly.

Digging trenches
In August 1942, these New Zealanders dug trenches to defend the patch of desert that they had won at the First Battle of El Alamein.

Combined forces
Thousands of Australians and New Zealanders, known as ANZACs, fought in Africa alongside soldiers from India, South Africa, and all over the British empire. During July 1942 and again in October, they fought the Germans for control of El Alamein, Egypt.

Into Africa
Allied supplies came along the Suez Canal or through the British territory Gibraltar. Axis supplies sailed into Tripoli, then trucked along the coast road.

Hard times
Desert conditions were tough. The days were blisteringly hot but the nights were cold. Vehicles and shell fire whipped up sandstorms, and the grit turned the tiniest scratches into painful sores. Food spoiled in the heat, dysentery was common, and water was too scarce to waste on washing.

Popular leader
Rommel (far left) inspired great respect from his troops. He lived, ate, and fought alongside his men, and cared for their welfare.

Sun goggles
Goggles blocked the sun and the windblown sand. Rommel had a favorite pair, which he captured from a British officer.

Eyewitness
NAME: Hans Klein
DATE: Born in 1921
FROM: Germany
DETAILS: Klein was a furniture maker before he joined the German forces. He served as a private in the Afrika Korps from 1942 to 1943 and was awarded the Iron Cross medal for bravery.

❝ Flies were a problem, and we had no control over them. Nets that we wore over our faces at all times protected us from the flies and allowed us to enjoy eating. To eat some bread with jelly, first you had to get all the flies off the bread and then quickly slip it under your net—hoping not to bring them all inside the net with you. ❞

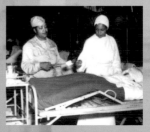

Medical care
Casualties were treated at field hospitals. The use of penicillin and blood transfusions saved millions of lives.

M4 Sherman

The United States shipped the first M4 tanks to North Africa in the late summer of 1942. At last the Allies had a fast-moving, fast-firing tank with the power to punch holes in German armored vehicles. The M4 was used in all theaters of war. The British called the newcomer the Sherman after the famous Civil War general.

Gunner
Second in command, this gunner operated the turret gun.

3 in. (75 mm) gun
The gun fired shells that could penetrate more than 2.5 in. (6 cm) of armor.

Driver's hatch
The driver's seat was raised so that he could look through this hatch when not under fire.

On track
More M4s were made than any other tank. Mass-produced at 11 different factories, they were used by British, Canadian, and Free French forces, as well as by the US military.

Browning machine gun
The twin .30-caliber machine guns came with 6,250 rounds of ammunition.

Hull machine gunner
This gunner was also the tank's co-driver and radio operator.

Stopping a tank

M24 GRENADE

In an attempt to halt these apparently unstoppable monsters, antitank guns fired armor-piercing shells or grenades, and land mines were planted ahead of an expected advance. In close-up battles, enemy soldiers dropped grenades inside the tanks.

ANTITANK MINE

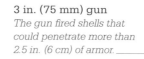

A.C.E.L.\nMle 1935

PZB 39 ANTITANK RIFLE

Driver's control levers
Levers were linked to the left and right tracks, which turned the tank.

Tank commander
He gave directions to the driver and chose targets for the gunners.

Turret casing
The iron turret was cast in one 3 in. (7.5 cm) thick piece for maximum strength.

Ammunition loader
His job was to take shells from the ammunition rack and load the turret gun by hand.

Turret
The electric motor–driven turret could turn in a full circle, unlike the turrets of other tanks.

Armor plating
This was 2 in. (5 cm) thick on the sides, but only 0.25 in. (6 mm) on top.

Engine
The gasoline-fueled, 400-horsepower engine was tilted to fit into the tank's shell.

Ammunition
The tank carried 90 rounds of 3 in. (75 mm) shells.

Drive shaft
The propeller shaft connected to the front-mounted transmission.

Wheels
Each track ran on 12 lower, 4 upper, and 2 rear wheels.

Suspension
A spring suspension system absorbed some of the bumps on rough ground.

Track
The 16.5 in. (42 cm) wide rubber tracks each had 79 "shoes."

49,230
Shermans were built— it was the main tank used by the Allies in World War II

Hot and noisy

The tank's crew members had to cope with the sweltering heat and deafening roar of the engine and gun; they used hand signals to communicate. Early Shermans caught fire easily when fired on, so crews reinforced the armor with extra metal sheets, timber, or sandbags. If they were hit, they scrambled out of an escape hatch underneath the vehicle.

M4A1 specifications	
Introduced	1941
Number made	49,230
Crew members	5
Weight (empty)	29.8 tons
Length	19 ft. 2 in. (5.8 m)
Width	8 ft. 7 in. (2.6 m)
Height	8 ft. 2 in. (2.5 m)
Range	120 mi. (193 km)
Top speed	28 mph (45 kph)
Fuel capacity	210 gal. (796 L)
Turret gun	3 in. (75 mm)

Spies and special ops

The most dangerous wartime missions were behind enemy lines. Spies risked their lives learning about troop movements, weapons development, and other sensitive information. Special forces attacked key targets such as supply lines.

Special ops

All sides had special operations (ops) units. Their operatives were trained in close combat so that they could kill an enemy guard in a prison or munitions factory without the noise of a gun raising an alarm.

Special Air Service
The British SAS was formed in July 1941 to attack behind German lines in North Africa. In one early mission, an SAS force blew up 60 German aircraft without a single British casualty.

Scouts and Raiders
Formed in the US in 1942, the Scouts and Raiders specialized in underwater reconnaissance. Many of their missions involved supporting troop landings.

Spy rings

All countries had intelligence agencies and spies. Many spies worked in counterespionage, or stopping enemy spies. Some were double agents who passed on false information.

US OSS
The Office of Strategic Services was the US's first spy agency; its staff was trained by the British secret services. It ran spy networks around the world and later became the CIA.

Founded:	1942
Operatives:	24,000
Known for:	Spying in Nazi Germany; supporting partisans against Japan

SPY: VIRGINIA HALL
US agent Hall worked in Vichy France for the SOE and then the OSS. She found sites where weapons for resistance fighters could be dropped, helped airmen who had been shot down escape, and reported on German troop movements. She was nicknamed "the Limping Lady" because of her wooden foot, the result of a hunting accident. Hall died in 1982 at age 76.

British SOE
The Special Operations Executive supported resistance movements in Europe and Asia. Its agents were trained in creating disguises, parachuting, weapons usage, unarmed combat, map reading, and radio communications.

Founded:	July 1940
Operatives:	13,000
Known for:	Helping resistance movements; feeding fake information to the Germans

SPY: JUAN PUJOL GARCIA
Spanish-born Garcia persuaded the Germans to take him on as a spy—but only because he wanted to work as a double agent. His sympathies lay with the British. Garcia gave the Germans fake information about D-Day, convincing them that the landings would take place farther up the coast. After the war, Garcia faked his own death and went to live in Venezuela.

German Abwehr
The Abwehr was the Wehrmacht's military intelligence bureau, loyal to Germany, not to Hitler. It was involved in an attempt on Hitler's life in 1944. The SD, a rival intelligence agency, reported to high-ranking Nazi Heinrich Himmler.

Founded:	1921
Operatives:	Number unknown
Known for:	Infiltrating a Dutch underground unit

SPY: ELYESA BAZNA
Bazna worked for the British ambassador in Turkey, but he was really a German spy, with the code name Cicero. Whenever the ambassador took a bath, Bazna opened a safe and photographed secret documents. The British later claimed that Bazna was a double agent. Double cross became triple cross after the war when Bazna realized that the Abwehr had paid him with counterfeit money.

Soviet GRU

Stalin did not trust anyone, so spies from the GRU, the main Soviet intelligence agency, infiltrated both Allied and Axis powers. GRU agents uncovered German battle plans crucial to the Soviet victory over Germany at the Battle of Kursk in summer 1943.

Founded: **1921**

Operatives: **Thousands (exact number unknown)**

Known for: **Stealing information on the atomic bomb**

SPY: RICHARD SORGE

Sorge was a German Communist who supported the Soviet Union. He worked as a journalist in Germany, where he joined the Nazi Party as part of his cover. He warned Stalin about Hitler's invasion plans in 1941 but was ignored. Sorge ran a spy network in Japan but was discovered by the Japanese and hanged in 1944. He has been called the greatest spy of all time.

Japanese spies

In Japan, all agents studied the martial art of aikido. Some learned Russian so that they could spy in the Soviet Union. Others scouted Pearl Harbor before the 1941 attack. Many aided local nationalists in Asia, who wanted freedom from western colonial rule.

Founded: **1938**

Operatives: **2,500**

Known for: **Finding weaknesses in Singapore's defenses**

SPY: VELVALEE DICKINSON

US-born Dickinson ran a doll-trading business in New York—but she was also a spy. Writing to an address in Argentina, she sold information to the Japanese. Her letters, intercepted by the FBI, seemed to be about dolls but were in code and actually detailed US naval ship repairs and movements. In 1944, Dickinson was found guilty of espionage and sentenced to ten years in jail.

Spy kit

Secret agents used a range of equipment, from simplistic to the latest technology. Their spy gear had to be easy to carry and conceal, but quick to work.

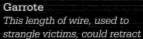

Garrote
This length of wire, used to strangle victims, could retract into the handle.

Concealed knife
The 5.5 in. (13.5 cm) blade was released by a button on the handle.

Cudgel
The weighted steel ball could be used to club someone on the head.

Multipurpose weapon

The McLaglen Peskett close-combat weapon was three weapons in one: a garrote (strangle wire), a knife, and a cudgel. Just 7 inches (18 cm) long, it was very easy to hide on the body, perhaps strapped to a leg.

Hidden blade

Blades were hidden in many ways—inside shoe heels, fake coins, or, in this case, an innocent-looking pencil. Blades were useful for cutting tires or wires, as well as people.

Pencil
The wood has been cut away to reveal the blade inside.

Modified Luger

This silenced Luger pistol was part of the kit intended to be used in the attempt to assassinate Hitler on July 20, 1944.

Silencer
The silencer muffled the bang of the gun.

Sure shot

This tiny camera, about 3.5 in. (9 cm) across, was seized from a spy after the war. Light, small, and easy to conceal, it could take pictures of documents at close range.

Victory in North Africa

The turning point of the war took place in North Africa. In late 1942, General Montgomery led the Allied forces across the desert. The Second Battle of El Alamein shocked Germany into retreat for the first time. Then, as British and US forces poured in, the African coast became the launchpad for an invasion of Italy that brought the battle back into Europe.

NORTH AFRICA, NOV. 1942–MAY 1943

ITALY
SPAIN
SICILY
TUNISIA
Tobruk   El Alamein
MOROCCO
ALGERIA
Sidi Barrani   EGYPT
LIBYA

African trap
After the Allied triumph at El Alamein, Allied forces stormed ashore in Morocco and Algeria, trapping Rommel in Tunisia. The surrounded Axis forces surrendered on May 13, 1943.

MAP KEY
━━ Allied fleet
━━ UK troops
━━ German troops

Second Battle of El Alamein

SEPT.– OCT. 1942 — Rommel laid 3 million mines across the front, in two 5-mile (8 km) belts. To trick Rommel about his tank positions, Montgomery placed dummy tanks to the south and disguised real tanks as trucks.

OCT. 23 — After a six-hour artillery barrage, the Allies advanced at night.

OCT. 24 — Montgomery's troops slowly cleared paths through the minefields for their advancing columns of tanks.

OCT. 25 — To the north, Australian troops captured a key German lookout post, Point 29.

OCT. 26 — British bombers sank a German oil tanker in the Mediterranean, off Tobruk, Libya, adding to Rommel's supply problems.

NOV. 2 — After a seven-hour artillery barrage, the Allies advanced, punching a 12-mile-wide (19 km) hole in the German lines.

NOV. 3 — The advancing Allies found enemy forces ready to surrender or already gone. The Germans left behind thousands of vehicles with empty fuel tanks.

NOV. 9 — Rommel's forces lost a key position at Sidi Barrani, in northwestern Egypt.

NOV. 11 — Despite Hitler's orders to stand and fight, the Axis forces retreated from Egypt. 25,000 had been killed or wounded, and a further 25,000 had been captured. The Allies suffered just 13,000 casualties.

"The battle is going very heavily against us. We're being crushed by the enemy weight"

—ERWIN ROMMEL, NOVEMBER 3, 1942

5.5 IN. (14 CM) ARTILLERY GUN, BRITISH

The crunch

Fought mostly at night, across a 40-mile-long (64 km) front in the Egyptian desert, the Second Battle of El Alamein halted the Axis advance toward the Middle East and sent the Germans into retreat. Having cracked German codes, the Allies knew that Rommel was ill and short on fuel. His 110,000 troops and 559 tanks were outnumbered by the Allies' 195,000 men and 1,351 tanks, including the new US Shermans.

Monty's men
Montgomery's army combined men from Britain, Australia, India, and New Zealand, as well as Free French forces. Thousands of Germans surrendered to them in Egypt.

Sicily and beyond

The Allies gathered a huge invasion force to cross the Mediterranean, and they began by attacking the island of Sicily. The Germans were not prepared, because they had found a planted body, floating in the sea off Spain, that carried plans of fake invasions. Sicily was captured in August 1943. The Allies invaded Italy on September 3, and Italy surrendered five days later. Germany fought on.

Over the waves

At dawn on July 10, 1943, a fleet of 2,590 ships transported 180,000 troops to the eastern and southwestern coasts of Sicily. In all, 450,000 Allied troops landed during the 38-day battle.

60,000:

the number of casualties suffered by
both sides at Monte Cassino

Battle of Monte Cassino

Occupied by German forces, the historic hilltop monastery of Monte Cassino, Italy, blocked the Allies' route north from southern Italy to Rome. The Allies attacked on January 17, 1944, but German troops were able to hold out until May 18.

A town in ruins

Intensive bombing and shelling wrecked Monte Cassino and the town below. Craters and rubble made perfect foxholes for the German defenders.

The
of th

* On which famous day did the Allies invade France?

* What happened after Germany surrendered?

* How did one Little Boy flatten a whole city?

end

e war

Path to peace

As the Allies pushed Nazi forces back to Berlin, some of the bloodiest battles of the war in Europe were fought. In the Pacific, Japan resisted stubbornly until the dropping of two atomic bombs forced its surrender.

FEB. 1945
Yalta
The heads of Britain, the US, and the Soviet Union met at the city of Yalta, in the Crimea (now Ukraine). They agreed to divide Germany into zones and to form the United Nations (UN), and Stalin promised to declare war on Japan.

CHURCHILL, ROOSEVELT, AND STALIN AT YALTA

DWIGHT EISENHOWER
US Army

Lived:	1890–1969
Rank in 1944:	Supreme commander of Allied forces in Europe
Nickname:	Ike

JUNE 6, 1944
D-Day
General Eisenhower landed the first of 2 million Allied troops on five beaches in Normandy, France, ready to push back the Germans. The invasion involved 4,000 landing craft, 1,200 warships, and 14,500 planes.

JAN. 27, 1944
At last, the survivors in the besieged Soviet city of Leningrad were freed.

JUNE 13, 1944
The first German V-1 flying bombs landed in England. Each "doodlebug" carried a 1,870 lb. (848 kg) warhead.

SEPT. 8, 1944
Germany targeted London with the first V-2 rockets.

•1944•

JULY–AUG. 1943
At Kursk, in the Soviet Union, the Soviets defeated the Germans in the largest tank battle ever. There were 6,500 tanks in the battle.

NOV. 1943
Meeting in Tehran, Iran, Roosevelt and Churchill promised Stalin that they would invade France the following May.

Dots represent monthly increases.

AUG. 25, 1944
Paris freed
General Dietrich von Choltitz surrendered Paris to the Allies. He had disobeyed Hitler's orders to destroy its monuments and bridges. The Allies arranged for a French-led division to march in to reclaim the capital city.

A VICTORY PARADE IN PARIS

DEC. 16, 1944
Final push
In a last-ditch offensive, the Germans attacked the Allies in northern France, making the Allies' front line bulge inward. The Battle of the Bulge lasted six weeks, but under Patton's leadership, the Germans were pushed back.

19,000:
the number of US soldiers who died in the Battle of the Bulge

GEORGE PATTON
US Army

Lived:	1885–1945
Rank in 1944:	General
Nickname:	Old Blood and Guts

B-17 FLYING FORTRESS

FEB. 13–15, 1945
Dresden bombing

British and US bombers dropped high explosives and firebombs on the previously untouched city of Dresden, Germany. The fires were so hot that they created 90 mph (145 kph) winds, and the roads melted. About 25,000 people died.

316:
the number of
Flying
Fortresses that flew in the raids over
Dresden

AUG. 14, 1945
Japan surrenders

Following massive US bombing raids on Tokyo from August 10 to 14, Emperor Hirohito announced Japan's surrender. The official surrender ceremony took place on September 2.

THE SURRENDER CEREMONY

MAY 7, 1945
In Reims, France, General Alfred Jodl surrendered German forces to the Allies.

JULY 26, 1945
The US, Britain, and China told Japan to surrender or face "utter destruction."

AUG. 6, 1945
A US uranium bomb destroyed the Japanese city of Hiroshima.

OCT. 24, 1945
The United Nations was founded with the aim of building world peace.

MAR. 24, 1945
Allied forces crossed the Rhine River and advanced into the heart of Germany.

•1945•   •1946

JAN. 17, 1945
Soviet forces captured the Polish capital, Warsaw, and freed it from German rule.

APR. 28, 1945
Mussolini was captured and shot, along with 13 others, by Italian partisans.

MAY 2, 1945
After a week of street fighting, the Red Army took control of Berlin.

NOV. 1945
A series of trials began in Nuremberg, Germany, to try Nazi leaders for war crimes.

News Chronicle
HITLER DEAD
Doenitz, new Fuehrer, says: We fight on

WEHRMACHT ORDERED TO MAINTAIN DISCIPLINE

All the generals must surrender

A BRITISH PAPER REPORTING HITLER'S DEATH

APR. 30, 1945
Hitler's suicide

As the Red Army advanced on Berlin, Hitler shot himself in the underground air-raid bunker complex that had been his home since January. Hours before he died, he married Eva Braun, who also committed suicide.

AUG. 9, 1945
Nagasaki

The US dropped a 14 lb. (6.4 kg) plutonium bomb on the Japanese port city of Nagasaki. The explosion killed at least 40,000 people, with tens of thousands more dying in the weeks and months that followed.

THE MUSHROOM CLOUD ABOVE NAGASAKI

D-Day

At dawn on June 6, 1944, Allied troops landed in France to start the attack on Hitler's armies across Europe. This was the scene on Omaha Beach, one of five landing points along a 50-mile (80 km) stretch of the Normandy coast. More than 158,000 men landed on D-Day itself, the first of a total invasion force of 2 million.

Battle of the Bulge

At the end of 1944, the Allied advance eastward across Europe toward Berlin seemed inevitable. Then, in December, the Germans launched a surprise attack that became known as the Battle of the Bulge. This offensive held up the advance for two months.

Still operational

The Allies destroyed the massive bunkers that were the secret launch sites for Germany's V-2 rockets. But the Nazis continued to launch V-2s from mobile units.

Deadly rockets

Through the winter of 1944–45, around 2,500 people in London alone were killed by V-2s, many of which were launched from country roads in northern Europe.

Stretched thin

The Allies' advance across war-ravaged Europe was filled with difficulties and terrors. The Germans had left mines and booby traps. Snipers hid in ruined buildings. The Allied commanders stretched their lines thin—the 80-mile (130 km) front in the Ardennes, between Belgium and France, was held by 60,000 US troops. When the Germans attacked, they did so with 200,000 men.

Slow progress

Soldiers had to use mine detectors to clear buildings that the retreating Germans had booby-trapped.

Into battle

Hitler wanted to split the British, Canadian, and US armies in the Ardennes, and block a key supply route. The US forces were pushed back, but Allied counterattacks and German fuel shortages ended the battle after six weeks.

The "bulge"
This map shows the bulge created by the advance of 200,000 German soldiers. They found a weak point in the Allied lines.

6 **January 25**
Weeks of counterattacks forced the Germans to halt the assault.

5 **December 23**
Better weather allowed Allied planes to fly 15,000 trips in 4 days to attack troops and supply lines.

4 **December 21**
German troops surrounded and besieged Bastogne, trapping 18,000 US troops.

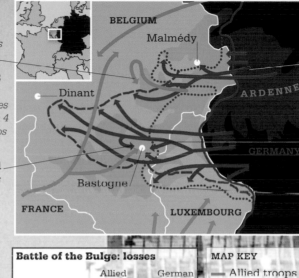

1 **December 16**
The Germans bombarded the Allies. Bad weather prevented a response.

2 **December 17**
German forces pushed both north and south.

3 **December 19**
The Germans had now created a bulge in the Allied lines.

BELGIUM
Malmédy
Dinant
ARDENNES
Bastogne
GERMANY
FRANCE
LUXEMBOURG

Battle of the Bulge: losses	Allied	German
Dead	20,876	15,652
Casualties	42,893	41,600
Captured or missing	23,554	27,582

MAP KEY

⎯ Allied troops	⎯ front line Dec. 16
⎯ German troops	···· front line Dec. 20
Allied territory	⎯ front line Dec. 25
German territory	

Icy warfare
Allied soldiers were forced to fight against almost overwhelming odds in the thick forests and narrow valleys of the Ardennes, in grueling weather. Here, a US Seventh Armored Division patrols the Belgian village of Saint Vith.

Eyewitness

NAME: Robert C. Cable

DATE: 1944

LOCATION: Belgium

DETAILS: From Cleveland, OH, Cable was a 19-year-old soldier in the US Army's Seventeenth Airborne Division. He described the Battle of the Bulge as "the worst Christmas I ever spent."

❝ The weather conditions were atrocious. We were losing 2,000 men a day, not to combat so much as to the weather. I mean frozen feet, frozen fingers, everything. We had a lot of problems with that. ❞

Berlin falls

In 1945, as Allied forces advanced on Berlin from east and west, Hitler stayed in his bunker. Stalin was determined to crush the German capital, so the other Allies held back as 2.5 million Red Army troops entered the city. The war in Europe was over, but in the Pacific and Asia, it continued for three more months.

Fall of Berlin

The Russians encircled Berlin and then captured it street by street. Out for revenge, they looted shops and robbed civilians. After Hitler's suicide, German generals eventually had no choice but to surrender.

Soviet advance
On April 30, 1945, Red Army tanks rumbled toward the Reichstag, the German parliamentary building.

Eyewitness

NAME: Dorothea von Schwanenfluegel

DATE: April 20, 1945

DETAILS: Polish-born Schwanenfluegel moved to Germany as a child. In 1945, she was a 29-year-old mother in Berlin.

❝ We noticed a sad-looking young boy across the street, standing behind some bushes in a self-dug, shallow trench. I went over to him and found a mere child in a uniform many sizes too large for him, with an antitank grenade lying beside him. Tears were running down his face, and he was obviously very frightened. . . . [H]e had been ordered to lie in wait here, and when a Soviet tank approached, he was to run under it and explode the grenade. ❞

Fall of Berlin: Time line

Apr. 16 *The Soviets began to bombard Berlin's outer defenses. German deserters were hanged from the trees.*

Apr. 20 *Hitler celebrated his birthday by decorating Hitler Youth boys with medals. The last Anglo-US air raid on Berlin took place.*

Apr. 26 *The Soviets had control of the suburbs. Marshals Zhukov and Konev were competing to claim Berlin.*

Apr. 30 *The battle for the Reichstag began. Hitler and his wife committed suicide. Joseph Goebbels was made chancellor.*

Tea for victory
At this celebratory tea party in London, children ate sandwiches and cake at a giant V-shaped table.

Victory and defeat

War-weary civilians and troops from Allied countries celebrated Victory in Europe (V-E) Day with street parties and dancing. But in German and Italian cities, people starved, as did many others in war-torn lands. Across Europe, 12 million refugees began the long journey home.

Eyewitness

NAME: Mollie Panter-Downes

DATE: May 19, 1945

DETAILS: Born in August 1906, Panter-Downes was an English novelist who wrote the Letter from London column for the *New Yorker* magazine.

❝ The government decided against sounding the sirens in a triumphant 'all clear,' for fear that the noise would revive too many painful memories. For the same reason, there were no salutes of guns—only the pealing of the bells, and the whistles of tugs on the Thames sounding the doot, doot, doot, dooooot of the 'V,' and the roar of the planes, which swooped back and forth over the city, dropping red and green signals toward the blur of smiling, upturned faces.❞

US celebrations
Jubilant crowds gathered in cities across the US, especially New York. They marked V-E Day with ticker-tape parades, cheering, singing, and triumphant flag-waving.

May 1 *Goebbels and his wife committed suicide after poisoning their six children. Admiral Dönitz became head of Germany.*

May 2 *General Weidling, in charge of Berlin's defenses, surrendered the city on the radio, saying: "Anyone who falls for Berlin dies in vain."*

May 4–5 *Thousands of German troops marched west to surrender to British and US forces rather than to the Soviets.*

May 8 *V-E Day: The Germans officially signed their surrender in Berlin, with Soviet, US, British, and French witnesses.*

Hiroshima

The Pacific war dragged on, and in the summer of 1945, the United States decided to force Japan to surrender by deploying a devastating new weapon: the atomic bomb. Its first target was the city of Hiroshima. When the Japanese did not surrender right away, a second bomb was dropped, on the city of Nagasaki. These powerful weapons produced blistering heat that killed instantly, and deadly radiation that caused death and suffering for years afterward.

AUG. 6

THE ATOMIC BOMB LITTLE BOY

2:45 AM — The B-29 bomber *Enola Gay* took off from the Pacific island of Tinian. Its deadly cargo was "Little Boy," the atomic bomb destined for Hiroshima.

8:15 AM — Little Boy was dropped on Hiroshima, a city of 300,000 people. A fireball 2,000 feet (600 m) in diameter engulfed everything. At least 70,000 people died instantly.

8:25 AM — The mushroom cloud billowed up to a height of 40,000 feet (12,190 m).

AUG. 9 — The atomic bomb "Fat Man" was detonated over Nagasaki. The blast killed at least 40,000 people.

AUG. 15 — Emperor Hirohito announced on the radio that Japan would surrender.

SEPT. 6 — After a month, 70,000 more citizens of Hiroshima had died from burns or radiation sickness.

"The enemy has begun to employ a new, most cruel bomb"

—EMPEROR HIROHITO'S SURRENDER SPEECH

The war in numbers

World War II was the biggest and most terrible war the world has ever seen. There were 61 countries involved, and 1.9 billion of their populations took up arms and fought. About 1 in every 40 people in the world died, many of them civilians. The war lasted so long because Germany and Japan stubbornly fought on even when it was clear that they could not win.

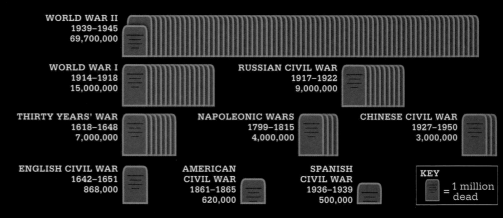

WORLD WAR II
1939–1945
69,700,000

WORLD WAR I
1914–1918
15,000,000

RUSSIAN CIVIL WAR
1917–1922
9,000,000

THIRTY YEARS' WAR
1618–1648
7,000,000

NAPOLEONIC WARS
1799–1815
4,000,000

CHINESE CIVIL WAR
1927–1950
3,000,000

ENGLISH CIVIL WAR
1642–1651
868,000

AMERICAN CIVIL WAR
1861–1865
620,000

SPANISH CIVIL WAR
1936–1939
500,000

KEY
= 1 million dead

WWII in context
When US president Woodrow Wilson took the United States into World War I in 1917, he called it "a war to end all wars." These casualty statistics show that, sadly, he was wrong.

Different styles
Previous wars were fought by armies charging at one another and fighting hand to hand. World War II was far more destructive.

War machine
The fighting on land, at sea, and in the air called for the production of enormous amounts of extra equipment. Factories in the United States supplied much of the Allied armory. They employed mass-production techniques and recruited 3 million women to work in special war factories, which tremendously boosted the workforce.

Decades of debt
These are some of the pieces of equipment shipped from US factories during World War II. The Allies took decades to pay back their debts.

650,000 jeeps

300,000 aircraft

89,000 tanks

2,751 cargo ships to Britain

3,000,000 machine guns

14,000,000 pairs of boots to Russia

World War II lasted

2,174 days

Horse sense
Horses were still important for transportation. Troops rode them, and they hauled artillery and other equipment on muddy and snowy routes that overwhelmed wheeled vehicles.

RUSSIA

GERMANY

FRANCE

KEY
= 1 million horses

At the front line
On the eastern front, most German artillery and supplies were horse drawn, and the Soviets had cavalry units.

The postwar world

With the major European nations weakened or needing aid after the war, countries that had been colonies left their European rulers or were encouraged to become independent. The age of empires was over. Communism gained influence as the balance of world power changed.

Independent India
Mahatma Gandhi's Quit India campaign helped end British rule in August 1947. India and the new state of Pakistan became independent.

Changes in Japan
The Japanese emperor lost all political and military power in 1947. Japanese women voted for the first time in the 1946 elections.

China turns Communist
In 1949, Mao Tse-tung won a three-year civil war and largely isolated China until 1976.

40 million:
the number of refugees in Europe when the war ended

Berlin conquered
The Red Army entered Berlin on April 21, 1945. They looted buildings and attacked many civilians in revenge for the devastation caused by the Nazis.

1947

The American Marshall Plan pumped $13 billion into European countries to support industry and agriculture.

1949

On April 4, Western powers fearful of Communist threats formed the North Atlantic Treaty Organization (NATO), a political and military peacekeeping alliance.

1951

The European Coal and Steel Community, a stepping stone to the European Union, was founded to join countries in an economic union and to make war less likely.

aircraft carrier
A large warship with a long, open deck from which aircraft can take off and on which they can land while at sea.

air raid
An attack by military aircraft, usually large groups of bombers.

air-raid shelter
A structure to protect people during air raids. This might be a basement, a tunnel, a shelter in the yard, or a subway station.

Allied forces
The 26 nations that fought against the Axis powers in World War II. Members included Great Britain, the Soviet Union, the United States, Canada, France, and China.

anti-Semitism
Prejudice against or hatred of Jews.

appeasement
The act of making undue concessions to satisfy the demands of someone greedy for power.

atomic bomb
A nuclear weapon that releases a huge amount of energy. It creates an enormous explosion and spreads harmful radiation.

Axis powers
In World War II, Nazi Germany, Fascist Italy, and Japan. Their alliance began in 1936 and lasted until their defeat in 1945.

blackout
A period of darkness in a city during an air raid (achieved by turning off or hiding all lights), to make it harder for enemy aircraft to find their targets.

Blackshirt
An armed member of a Fascist group founded in Italy by Benito Mussolini in 1919. Blackshirts were named for their uniforms.

Blitz
The devastating nighttime bombings of Britain and Northern Ireland by the German Luftwaffe from September 1940 to May 1941. The main targets were large cities and ports.

blitzkrieg
A military maneuver in which the attacking army moves very fast and is supported by tanks and aircraft. *Blitzkrieg* is a German word meaning "lightning war."

chaff
Thousands of tiny strips of tinfoil, dropped from planes to produce a confusing image on enemy radar screens. This made incoming planes hard to spot.

cipher
A way of hiding the meaning of a message by changing its letters.

civilian
Someone who is not on active duty in the armed services.

colony
A country or region ruled by another country.

Communism
A set of beliefs about how society should be run, based on the idea that everyone should be treated the same and all property should be shared.

concentration camp
A large compound where civilians, especially Jews, were kept in very harsh conditions. In some camps, also known as extermination or death camps, the prisoners were deliberately killed.

convoy
A fleet of ships or group of vehicles traveling together, often protected by an escort of warships or armed troops.

D-Day
A military term short for *day day*—the chosen day for a particular event. Specifically, *D-Day* now refers to June 6, 1944.

democracy
A political system in which people vote to elect leaders to govern their country. Equality and freedom are important in a democracy.

destroyer
A small, fast warship that attacks enemy ships with weapons such as guns, torpedoes, and depth charges.

dictator
A person who rules with absolute power and without effective opposition. Even if a dictator is elected, this person usually rules by force.

dive-bomber
An aircraft that dives quickly and steeply toward a target

to drop its bombs from up close. This strategy makes it hard to counterstrike with antiaircraft fire.

dogfight
A violent air battle between two or more fighter planes.

dugout
A pit dug into the ground, where soldiers can take shelter while firing on the enemy.

empire
A group of nations ruled by an emperor or other powerful sovereign, or by a government. Britain, France, and other European countries had empires that included colonies in Africa and Asia.

Fascism
A system of government that is led by a dictator who has absolute power and believes that this nation or race is superior to others.

Final Solution
A Nazi government program that intended to kill millions of Jews and other "inferior" peoples who were considered to be enemies of Germany.

foxhole
A small pit dug by soldiers to provide shelter from enemy fire.

Free French
Members of the organized movement to continue warfare against Germany after France's

2,000 strips of foil can appear to be a B-17 bomber on a radar screen

Glossary

1940 defeat in World War II. Led by General Charles de Gaulle, the Free French eventually managed to unify most of the resistance forces in France.

fuselage
The main body of an aircraft, which holds crew and cargo and to which the wings and tail are attached.

gas mask
Equipment, worn over the face, that is fitted with a filter to clean the air that the wearer breathes. Gas masks are worn as protection from gas attacks.

Geneva Conventions
A series of articles that describe how injured soldiers and POWs should be treated. The first convention was introduced in 1864; Japan and the Soviet Union did not sign the 1929 convention.

genocide
The systematic murder of many people from the same racial or cultural group.

ghetto
A section of a city, often a highly populated slum area, where Jews were made to live by the Nazis during World War II.

Great Depression
The economic crisis that began with the Wall Street Crash in 1929. It spread worldwide and continued through the 1930s.

grenade
A small shell, full of explosives, that can be thrown by hand or fired from a rifle or other device.

hell ship
A Japanese ship carrying Allied POWs crammed into the holds, with little to eat or drink.

Hitler Youth
The organization set up in Germany by Adolf Hitler to educate and train children ages 13–18. There were two separate groups: one that prepared boys to be soldiers, and one that prepared girls to be mothers.

Holocaust
The mass murder of millions of Jews and other minority groups by the Nazis in concentration and death camps.

ideology
A set of ideas and beliefs that is shared by a nation, a political system, or a group of people.

incendiary
A shell, bomb, or grenade that is designed to start fires.

internment camp
A camp for civilian prisoners of war. The US government forced about 110,000 Japanese Americans into internment camps during World War II.

kamikaze
Relating to a Japanese tactic during World War II in which a pilot deliberately killed himself by flying his explosives-filled aircraft into a target, such as an enemy ship. *Kamikaze* means "divine wind."

Luftwaffe
The German air force. *Luftwaffe* means "air weapon."

marine
A soldier who is based on a warship but who also fights on land when necessary.

mine
An explosive device that is intended to injure or damage a person, tank, or ship. Land mines are hidden on or under the ground. Naval mines float on or just under the surface of the water.

Morse code
A way of sending messages using short and long signals, often called dots and dashes. Morse code can be sent as sounds or flashes of light.

munitions
Any weaponry used in combat, such as bombs, missiles, and mines, as well as ammunition.

nationalist
A person who is devoted to his or her nation and who may believe that it is better off being ruled independently and acting alone. Extreme nationalists may believe that their nation is superior to other nations or groups of people.

Nazi
A member of Hitler's National Socialist Party in Germany, which promoted racist, authoritarian ideas. *Nazi* is short, in English, for the German word *Nationalsozialismus*.

pact
An agreement or treaty between two or more nations that brings benefits to all sides.

partisan
A member of an armed resistance group fighting for and in his or her occupied country.

Phony War
The period at the beginning of World War II, from September 1939 to May 1940, after Britain and France had declared war on Germany. There was almost no fighting on land, but the nations were preparing for combat.

Polish Home Army
A resistance movement in Poland that fought against Nazi and Soviet occupation during the war.

Gas masks were issued for free in Britain; most Germans had to pay

prisoner of war
A person who is captured and held by the enemy during a war. Most POWs are members of the armed forces.

propaganda
Information that is distributed to help or mislead people. During wars, governments use propaganda to encourage their citizens or misinform the enemy.

radar
A system that sends out pulses of radio waves to locate the positions of objects, such as planes and ships. Radar stands for *RAdio Detecting And Ranging*.

radiation
A form of energy released by an atomic bomb. Radiation is very harmful to humans.

rationing
The act of controlling the amount of food and other basic items when a war has caused shortages. Gas, certain foods, clothing, and rubber were rationed in the United States during World War II.

reconnaissance
The study of an area to gather information about the position and resources of an enemy.

Red Army
The Soviet army, formed in February 1918. The army was increased in size in 1933 to combat the threat from Nazi Germany.

Red Cross
An international organization founded in Switzerland in 1863 to help victims of conflict. It sent 36 million aid parcels during World War II.

refugee
A person who has to flee their home because of persecution or war. Millions of people became refugees during World War II.

Reich
A German empire. The First Reich was the Holy Roman Empire (800–1806). The Second Reich was the German Empire (1871–1918). Hitler named his regime the Third Reich (1933–45).

sabotage
The deliberate damaging of equipment or operations in order to hinder an enemy during war.

shrapnel
The fragments of metal left after an explosion. British children collected pieces of shrapnel from bomb sites as souvenirs.

siege
An offensive in which troops surround a city so that no people, food, or supplies can get in or out. Sieges can last for months or even years.

sniper
A skilled shooter who fires on enemy soldiers from a hiding place, sometimes from a long distance away.

sonar
A system that sends out pulses of sound, then uses the returning echoes to detect and locate objects underwater. *Sonar* stands for *SOund NAvigation Ranging*.

stalag
A German POW camp. The largest, Stalag VII-A, held 130,000 Allied soldiers.

swastika
An ancient cross-shaped symbol, adopted as the Nazi Party's symbol in 1920. It then became Germany's national emblem in 1935.

torpedo
A self-propelled underwater missile that explodes when it hits or gets close to a target. Torpedoes were the main weapons used by submarines and U-boats.

Vichy France
The regime in the unoccupied southern part of France, which was allowed to govern itself after the German occupation of northern France in June 1940. Germany took over Vichy France in November 1942.

war bond
A government-issued savings bond, sold to raise money during a war. People give money to a government to buy bonds; the government promises to pay the money back, with interest, after the war ends.

Wehrmacht
The armed forces of the German Third Reich from 1935 to 1945.

The Welbike
This ingenious motorized bike was used on D-Day. It weighed only 75 lb. (34 kg), yet it could carry a paratrooper in full gear. It was designed to fit in a canister that could be dropped by parachute.

Index

Index